A
Camino
of the
Soul

Learning to Listen
When the Universe Whispers

KATHARINE ELLIOTT

ACKNOWLEDGEMENTS

With immense thanks to my life sisters Cheryl and Helen for their eyes, their candor and their love with this book. You will never know how much I truly appreciate you both!

To my Camino family, especially Liz, Paul, and Guy. Your humor, love and support made this adventure the Camino of my dreams. I am so very thankful we had each other! And to Maidere. That you listened to my stories and encouraged me to follow Jeannie's words: "Start writing..." brought it all into focus. Thank you!

Wendy Hall, my editor; you took my words and gently applied your technical expertise and sound advice. Thank you!

Thank you Heidi Sutherlin, for giving this memoir a face with your brilliant cover design.

To Chandler Bolt and the SPS team—WOW! You opened the door with your brilliant Self-Publishing School program. I am forever grateful

And to my Mom. You will never know how important hearing you say you are proud of me for following this calling has meant. I love you—Your Kathy girl.

CONTENTS

DEDICATION

With love to my son, Gregory, whose support and encouragement of his wandering Mom through these years has touched my heart.

And to my amazing sister, Mary, whose unwavering love and belief in me and in this project has kept me going. You are so loved!

INTRODUCTION

In 2014, I walked the Camino Santiago de Compostela in northern Spain. I walked after knowing for over two years that I would walk. When people asked why, all I could say was, "*I am supposed to.*" Their puzzled faces were nothing compared to the confusion in my own mind. Yet I knew deep in my being that this Camino, this 500-mile walk across northern Spain following in the footsteps of centuries of pilgrims before me, was mine to walk. It was a deep *soul knowing* which made no logical sense based on my current life commitments or finances. *It just was.*

This *knowing* took place in the fall of 2011. It had been a year during which I had spent several months with my Mom as she battled the decisions, and inevitably the surgery, she would face in learning she had a very aggressive form of breast cancer. It was also the year I realized the inevitable: my marriage was crumbling and would not survive without a new outlook. I needed a new perspective.

In the summer of 2011, I started reading. Our small outdoor garden in Rovinj, Croatia became my sanctuary. Dr. Wayne Dyer, Anita Moorjani, and Gregg Braden became daily companions. My paperback version of *The Power of Intention* was frayed after three readings, and my poor Sony E-book was locked onto *Dying to Be Me* and *Deep Truths.*

What happened was an awakening. In a short time, I understood that there is no *then and now, here or there...*everything is happening at once and time is not a linear continuum. And I came to believe there are no coincidences. I now understood the saying "the teacher appears when the student is ready." Often in the most fascinating of ways!

Late in the summer of 2011, my copy of Paulo Coelho's *The Pilgrimage,* his tale of walking El Camino, appeared. That I happened upon it hidden in the back of a dusty bookshelf intrigued me. Reading his words a second time, this ancient trek called to me.

That summer, I opened my thoughts to the possibilities that life as we see it is simply a fraction of what is taking place in our Universe. I came to understand that messages are sent in many ways if we but watch and listen. Synchronicities such as Coelho's book no longer surprised me. What also no longer surprised me was the validation and guidance we can receive from our angels.

I had believed since my mother-in-law's passing, a woman I dearly loved as family and *friend,* that the energy of our souls continues to cross boundaries after death. Difficult to comprehend, this communication can come to us in a variety of ways. She taught me that Angels exist!

By early 2012, I committed that I would indeed walk the Camino. By that time, my sister Jeannie who had passed away of pancreatic cancer in December of 2007 and my Aunt Mary Jo who died in February of 2012, had made their way to me. Angels surrounded me! And my belief in their abilities to guide, as well as my new-found belief that we can co-conspire *with* the Universe, were my operating status quo.

And so it was set. Fall of 2014 was the timeframe for my walk. In April of that same year, the faltering, maybe healing, marriage tumbled. Without the specifics which are not important here, my husband and I both knew it was over. How interesting the timing of the Universe! I would be walking the Camino as my marriage was ending...when I likely needed solitude the most!

In September of 2014, I followed my heart...followed my soul's call...and began the Camino Frances from St Jean Pied de Port in the French Pyrenees to Santiago de Compostela in northwest Spain. The experience of my trek was completely and utterly joyful. It reaffirmed my belief, an unquestioning understanding that the Universe will conspire on my behalf if I just flow with it...*if I simply let it.* Everything in my life was happening in undeniable precision...nothing in my life was out of order. And my angels were with me, teaching and guiding.

Beyond all else, these last remarkable four years of my life have taught me to *listen*. Listen to the energies of the Universe. Listen to the knowledge my soul cradles deep within. Listen to the love and guidance of my guardian angels...believe that all I need to know, all I need to understand, is available to me if I simply remain open to the forces of the Universe and listen.

As I write this, well over a year since that magnificent Camino experience, my soul's knowledge that I am to continue to walk far away trails has taken me to the southern reaches of Patagonian Chile and Argentina. I have traveled to remote reaches of the Scottish Highlands. In the fall of 2015, I walked a 200-mile portion of the famed Via Francigena in Italy, the ancient pilgrimage walk from Canterbury to Rome.

Guiding messages from my angels, along with the belief and understanding that the Universe truly conspires *with* us when we allow ourselves to surrender, have led me here to this book: **A Camino of the Soul Learning to Listen When the Universe Whispers.**

CHAPTER ONE

Sis

*Until she died, angels had not spoken to me. Until I
lost her, knew I would never hear her loved voice
again, I didn't believe they could. She taught me to
listen...to watch...she taught me angels guide.*

*Her lesson to me:
Listen to the whispers—we are here!*

Sis, a lifelong nickname for Sibylle, was my mother-in-law. More importantly, she had become a best friend. A friend chosen over the years as we did the female dance of protective mom of an only son and the chosen woman in his life—me. In the beginning we had laughed, played, partied - our relationship was enviable. We enjoyed each other's company and relished our time together.

As time went by, it became clear to her that I was not going anywhere. He and I were not a young fling; we were not two silly kids whose attraction would die a quiet death. Her son had fallen in love. Another woman would come before her. He had chosen me and would choose me over her if put to the test. Of course, I recognized there was no need for this, moms and daughters-in-law are not supposed to compete for a son/husband's affections. But it happens. She was jealous and was afraid of losing him. She shunned him.

Years later, she and I would share knowing smiles and squeeze each other's hands, recognizing the game of tug-of-war we had played. Her, desperately afraid of losing the boy she had raised; the young man who had become her party partner as he grew to adulthood, her confidant in all matters financial, her 'sitting at the kitchen table with a bottle and reliving old times' buddy.

And me, recognizing their single mom/only child relationship, trying to honor that bond. Yet somewhere, somewhere deep in my being, wondering at the role I saw him play, one she encouraged and a role he had grown up knowing. Neither knew any different. This is who they had become. Psychologically I may have known this, yet emotionally I still fought her, secretly heartened at some level that I was at least no longer watching their dance. She was angry. She made it clear she did not approve of me and she stayed away. Her son had made his choice, and it was me.

And yet, over time, the love sent her way via letters and cards as she battled a return of colon cancer for a third time, and his continued attempt at weekly calls overseas to her, finally touched her heart. Within two years, the war was over and a warm and loving friendship—a *'we are chosen girlfriends'* kind of friendship—grew between she and I.

Visits to Germany, her homeland, were joyous times. Our annual vacations were headed abroad to spend time with Sis. And, as the final bout of cancer attacked in 2004, he and I would split vacation times so more visiting could occur. A week in the spring for him, a week in the summer for me, and so forth. It worked. And, during those one-on-one times, she and I grew even fonder of one another, strengthening our friendship.

During the summer of 2005, it became apparent that she would soon need full-time care. Twice in the early spring months, icy Munich sidewalks still taking their toll on pedestrians, she had taken falls. No broken bones appeared, but the increased unsteadiness on her feet made it clear it was time to think about future care. A typically proud German woman, the idea of someone in her home was unfathomable. No one was going to do her cleaning, help with personal hygiene, or any other such foolishness! She was *not* having it. She was determined to carry on, albeit with more care when out and about. She was *not* going anywhere. She would stay right where she was, in the home she had lived in these past twenty years.

Early October came, and that wish had to be released. With all three of her children living in the States (Jack has a brother and sister who grew up with their father and stepmom) and no family there in Munich, it became a simple choice: stay in Munich and live in a senior care facility, potentially a nursing home or hospice as the cancer progressed, or come and live with Jack and I in the States. All four of us flew to Munich hoping to bring her back with us.

Jack and I knew this might happen when we bought our current home. The potential of having his Mom with us was very much taken into consideration during the home shopping process. Rambler style, with a guest bedroom and en suite bath were non-negotiables. That we found our dream home, in the perfect neighborhood, with glorious Puget Sound water views, was a gift! In bringing Sis to live with us she would have comfort, beautiful Pacific Northwest surroundings, and a home where her other children could come and spend quality time as she lived out her final three or four months.

It was perfect. And, she agreed quickly. Five days later we were on a plane and bound for the States—her final home with us.

I share all of this to help explain just how interconnected Sis and I became. Shortly after coming home, we had reached the point of twenty-four-hour care. Leaving her during the day as Jack and I continued with careers was not going to work. Bringing in someone unknown to help added an immense sense of pressure. Sis, while so ill, was dealing with new surroundings and feeling vulnerable, and Jack simply abhorred the idea of a stranger in his home. After much discussion, soul searching and, of course, financial finagling, we decided I would leave my career and stay home to care for Sis during these final months. It made practical sense but, more importantly, it was the *right* thing to do.

Let me back up a month or two and share what happened when we convinced Sis to let us find an oncologist here in Seattle after her arrival in October. We had her records from Munich, we had the pain relieving syringes of morphine issued by her doctors in Munich, and Jack was delicately administering those injections each day as directed by her German physicians. We brought this information with us on our first visit to the chosen oncologist. With some language translation, a review of new images he had ordered before he saw her, and the help of his wife who was a cancer researcher at a local university, he determined a more detailed diagnosis of her cancer type. And, with that, offered a possible drug to slow the tumor's growth gaining valuable time. It was a trial drug meant for another type of tumor, but given their similarity, he thought it might work.

He was a gift to our family. The drug did slow the tumor growth, and Sis gained another eighteen months of life that no one had expected. There were routine doctor visits and many days spent in bed with little to no energy, but for the most part, she regained a decent quality of life. Wandering the aisles of our local supermarket, shopping with me for favorite seafood, local bar haunt visits and social gatherings, even an excursion to the ocean for a four-day pre-Christmas shopping extravaganza, life had been regained. And through all of this, day in and day out, it was her and I.

Over those months, we shared even more intimate details about each other's lives. She knew my fears. She knew the challenges of my marriage (I didn't have to share—she saw). She knew of my past lives and I knew of hers. She understood the difficult choice I had made in letting my son's Dad take residential custody—she had done the same with her elder two. Two women brought together by a marriage, friends chosen by one another out of love and mutual respect. Who knew all those years ago, during the years of the war dance, we would be here.

We discussed the intricacies of her family, her sorrows and her joys with her children, and those precious early years she had spent with their father. We discussed politics over glasses of chardonnay for me, scotch and Coke for her. On good days, she and I hunkered down in the kitchen preparing an evening meal together. Cook a little, take a break, and sit outside. Sip a little. Head back in and prepare a bit more. If Paula Deen and the Barefoot Contessa can do it— and believe me, after hours of watching the Food Network on the not-so-good days, we knew all their tricks—then so could we!

There were so many full and rewarding days. We even

contemplated my return to work. She seemed to be getting better! Would our three loved doggies, Pepe, Gurly, and Lucky be enough company? Did she feel safe in what seemed an enormous house to her after years in European apartment style homes? Her hours of contemplation on the question, our three-way discussions, cocktails in hand, sitting on the patio staring out at the serene waters of Puget Sound, and yes, YES! She was physically strong enough and felt safe enough for us to be out of the house those eight or so hours each day. I would head back to work.

As often happens with cancer, it retreats, hiding beneath nooks and crannies in the body, leading us to believe it has given up the fight. And then one day—pounce; stray cat on a field mouse.

Play a little; toss around the body. Little mouse makes a shudder, gathers any strength left and tries for a run.

Slap! Paw down securely--there is no escape. Tear at the insides...eat at the brain...take over all control. Devour...death...done.

The birds were chirping just outside the bedroom window. Did they know? 5:14 a.m. on a summer morning. My beloved Sis, my chosen friend and confidant, let go quietly. Jack sat at her side speaking to her in German, her native tongue. He reminded her of girlfriends waiting on the other side with champagne and Rummikub tiles. She smiled...she was gone.

CHAPTER TWO

The 11's

"When you listen with your soul, you come into rhythm and unity with the music of the Universe"
~ John O'Donohue

7:11...the coffee pot blinked at me as I stumbled around the kitchen corner. Odd. I'd seen 7:11 on that clock at least three times in the last few days.

Sis had died just a couple weeks prior. I missed her terribly. The house carried the somber feel of a mortuary. Our three sweet lovable dogs were on edge. The air felt heavy...tired. After all, it was right down the narrow hallway, in her bedroom, that we kissed her goodbye; dressed her in clothes she had chosen a few days earlier and rubbed lotion on her hands one last time.

Phone calls to family and friends, tears, exhausted laughter recalling humorous moments in those last days.

Doesn't the shock of death, even an expected and welcomed death, trick us to laughter? Survival of our own spirits, I suppose. Five hours later after we had shared memories, brushed her hair one last time, and tipped a beer in her honor, the drivers arrived and she was gone. Wheeled to the waiting hearse in the driveway. Goodbye Sis. You are loved.

One week after Sis died, I got a phone call from my middle sister Jeannie. A severe backache, one she had been battling for several months I later learned, had now been diagnosed. Jeannie had pancreatic cancer. She had been in for X-rays two days earlier and now had the results. Would I please come over? She wanted to talk; she wanted me to be with her. Would I act as health care provider? Her time was limited, and it was likely there was nothing to be done.

I remember standing in our bedroom, my bright glorious bedroom, looking out over a vibrantly colored front garden. It was July. The wild roses were in bloom, iris stood brilliantly wrapped in their lavender shawls of color. The floor disappeared...I dropped. No...Nooooo!

Jeannie and I spent the next evening at her home. After initial tears as I hugged her upon arriving, we pulled ourselves together and headed to the grocery store. Wine and snack foods. Stock the larder; we were going to make this conversation tonight as easy as possible. So we drank. And we talked...for hours. What had she been thinking? Should I call the oncologist who had cared for Sis so brilliantly? We cried.

When would she tell her teenage children and how? And should she talk with their dad first? Of course. And what did she want me to do? I would do anything to ensure any of her wishes were met and fulfilled...yes, I promise!

Health care provider, please. She asked if I would please be her health care provider. I had just gone through this process. I knew what to do and who to talk to. Would I help her figure out the who, what, where, when, and why? Those were her wishes.

Midnight sitting outside her small home. The sky was clear. A multitude of stars shone in the heavens—her heaven. Tears. The air was warm as we listened to neighbors chatting across the yard. July summer in Seattle. We sat side by side huddled on the stoop as I promised to be there...as I promised to take care of her and help her to die in whatever way she chose. That night we slept curled on her bed together...sisters...cuddled...fending off the death man.

Two days later, 7:11 as I reached to grab the ringing phone. No one there.

Later, coffee cups washed and draining, I glanced at the clock...8:11.

I cannot say the moment when I understood, knew in my soul, that the coincidental glances at clocks with :11 timing was not coincidence at all. Sis was reaching out to let me know she was with me. She may no longer be a part of my physical world, but she was definitely here and signaling me. To put it to the test, because I am a logical woman after all, I asked her. I asked her to make it so abundantly clear that I could not doubt, could not conceive of questioning, what I was understanding. I wanted it so clear that when the time came to share this with my husband, a doubting man in all things spiritual, he would not guffaw.

Later that same night while watching TV with Jack, the time flashed on the screen: 7:11. Climbing into bed and reaching to set an alarm: 10:11. The next morning: 7:11 blinking on the coffee pot once again.

Ok! I accept. I believe you are here and I know you are staying close. PLEASE help me with Jeannie. I am so scared for her...for me. Help me to know what I should do.

During the next few days, Jeannie and I went to the cancer center where more detailed X-rays showed a metastasis of the cancer into all of her vital organs. She was given her sentence: four to six months. She took the verdict with such bravery. She would move to an apartment closer to her children who lived with their Dad, and she would be as active in their lives as possible. She would choose to *live* these months she had as best as she could.

Time flew during the next few weeks. We got her settled into her new apartment. We met the oncologist who would help with pain treatment until hospice was called and she tried to enjoy the last late days of summer.

And all the while I talked with Sis:

"Tell me what to do. What can I do to help? Am I giving her all she needs from me?"

And almost daily without fail, for 10 days straight, 7:11 came into my view. Clocks, license plates, page numbers...711. She was telling me something...what?

And then, as quickly as it had started in July, in those days directly following her death, Sis's spirit seemed to disappear. Now, as time passed, as the cancer took over Jeannie's body, I saw 11s less and less.

As the summer weeks rolled through fall, she lost weight. She became weak. Her desire to see family was less and less. Perhaps a desire to have her siblings and parents remember her as she had been, a beautiful, perky, and vivacious woman. Perhaps simply not choosing to hear anyone else's thoughts on what she should or should not do with her remaining time. I am not sure. What was difficult is I was not able to convince her otherwise when it came to family. She would do this *her* way, and I had promised to honor her wishes.

Toward the end of October, Sis surfaced again; 7:11 became as much of my daily life as it had been back in July. What did it mean? It had to mean something. I knew it was a specific message I was to understand.

On the fifth of November, it hit me. Jack and I were having a goodbye drink at a favorite pub. He and his brother were flying to Spain later in the day, beginning the search for what we hoped would be our new overseas home sometime the following year. Years of illness and death had shown us clearly that life was meant to be lived. Dreams were meant to be followed. They were the search committee while I stayed close to Jeannie.

Jack knew of the 7:11 messages although I think he still thought me a tad odd. I don't think he could quite conceive of communication from someone who had died, even if it was his Mom to me, her best friend.

On November fifth, it suddenly became so clear—711 was a date—11/7 except a German woman, as Sis was, would use the 7/11 version. It was a date, and it was in two days! Something significant would happen with Jeannie in two days' time. I had no doubt. A serene calm settled after initial tears of excitement at having solved the puzzle. She has been signaling November seventh.

Later that evening after kissing the guys goodbye at the airport and sending them on their way, I seriously contemplated booking kennel reservations for our three dogs. I was so sure I would be needed away from the house. Yet, my logical rational brain kept playing devil's advocate.

Kate, really? Messages from Sis...you're smarter than that. This is all coincidence. Should I book space; shouldn't I? Decide in the morning.

My cell phone buzzed. It was a text coming through.

"Touchdown Europe!"

A message the guys had landed safe and sound. Time on the text: 6:11 a.m. Lying there, I began questioning again.

Okay Sis, if tomorrow IS a vital day, please make it clear. No questions type of clear!

18

Next text, "Touchdown Valencia" 9:11 a.m.

A call to the kennel confirmed they could take the dogs for as long as I needed. I assumed that whatever this next day was to bring, it would pull me away from home. Better to make sure they would be in good hands. And I waited.

No phone calls that night. I checked in. Brian, Jeannie's best buddy, was with her and she was doing okay. Sleeping a great deal and not eating, but no changes. Medications were keeping her comfortable. Was I still taking her to her doctor appointment tomorrow? Yes...tell her I'll pick her up at 9 a.m.

The blow hit me in the stomach. Driving home from the doctor's, talking general chitchat as much as possible; out of the blue in the tone of a busy curt businesswoman she spoke.

"Katy, I have something to tell you. I don't want you to be my health care person any more, I want Brian to make all the decisions. I trust him. I don't want to see family. I don't trust you with that. Brian will be in charge. You take your direction from him. He will do what I want. You have to follow his orders. You do what *he* says."

Done. No conversation. This was a directive.

Boom! Her words, sharp and curt, cut through me. Stunned, I drove on in silence. In one swift instant Jeannie had opened the door, welcoming me to what I would later see as my greatest lesson, my toughest test. She was teaching unconditional love. That is what was required to carry on. I loved her dearly, and now to follow her wishes would require the truest of loves—711, November 7th, the date the test began.

Family members wanting to see Jeannie were held at abeyance as Brian followed her directive. She did not wish to see anyone other than her children, myself, friend Brian and her ex-husband, still a treasured love in her life. The next month would prove emotionally exhausting as the juggling between honoring her wishes as I had promised, wishes no doubt clouded by the pain-killing morphine, and my moral responsibility to my family members collided.

Unconditional love: a love which has no bounds and is unchanging regardless of life decisions, a difference in strong beliefs, an argument; affection without limitations.

This last month of Jeannie's life, she blessed many in our family with lessons in unconditional love. She was teaching even as she was dying. Loving her in this way was so terribly difficult given the circumstances, given the heartache and sense of loss at a sister and a daughter who did not want to allow goodbyes.

Sis knew. In death, the soul is everywhere at once. Time and space are nonexistent. Energy of the dead crisscrosses the matrix of dimensions instantaneously. Sis knew from her new realm and she alerted me. Her messages, not so much to prepare me for that specific day, but to teach me that if I listen, if I pay attention, I can hear my angels speak. They are present and watching and...if we pay close attention...they can be a guiding force all the days of our human physical existence. Once we believe...once we listen.

CHAPTER THREE

Change the Way You Look at Things...

"I confidently walk into my next step knowing that the same forces who guided me here will continue to be with me every moment." ~ *Charles Virtue*

It was the summer of 2011.

Jack and I had followed our European dream three years earlier. Careers left behind, the gorgeous dream house sold. We had anticipated a move to Spain when we started this overseas adventure. That idea, as much as we loved Spain, was not to be. Where did we land? Rovinj, Croatia.

Croatia, not yet a part of the European Union, had different extended visa requirements. Our immense efforts to obtain the necessary visas for overseas living in Spain had proven fruitless. Croatia's requirements were much less strict, offering an avenue for our dream to become reality. In the summer of 2008, we made the move.

The story of the move itself can be saved for another time. Suffice it say that an adventure of that magnitude breathed life back into our marriage, at least for a brief time. We purchased a condo, had it built out (apartments in new complexes came with bare walls, electricity, and not much else). The process of creating our new home was immensely enjoyable. Being within a few hours' drive to favorite locales—Munich, Venice, and Ljubljana—not to mention exploring our new home area, made for many happy months together.

As with all temporary diversions, the true issues remain. And ours did. Alcohol and a lack of emotional and physical intimacy, issues haunting us over our years together, continued to tear at us. Perhaps too much time on our hands in an early retirement; perhaps a desire to grow into something more on my part, perhaps a combination. What mattered was that if we did not get professional help, or at least a new way to view our marriage, it would crumble. By the summer of 2011, I found myself delving into self-help and motivational books in an attempt to find a new way to view us...to view my world. To accept my marriage as it was.

Our tiny European lawn overlooked a communal garden ripe with the aroma of fragrant lavender. Towering Italian cypress trees stretched to the clouds. Summer breezes blowing across the cool waters of the Adriatic Sea crossed our medieval village below. I would spend my summer in this sacred area outside my sliding door.

If this marriage was to survive I must learn a new way to view it; focus on all the good that is this man I love and refuse to be affected by his unwillingness to take part. I must accept him as he is, or leave.

"If you change the way you look at things, the
things you look at change." ~ Dr. Wayne Dyer

For the next months, I delved into the teachings of Wayne Dyer's *The Power of Intention, Change Your Thoughts—Change Your Life,* and *Wishes Fulfilled.* Focused on discovering a new perspective, his words spoke to me.

"You create your thoughts, your thoughts
create your intentions and your intentions
create your reality."

The Universe is energy and we are all a part of that source. One master consciousness of which we are each a piece. I am connected to all I see in this physical world and all that has been. In reading authors and ways of thinking totally new to me, I began to understand more clearly the mechanics of how Sis reached to me from beyond with her numeric messages, guiding when I asked for help. Energy—pure and simple. It is all about energy.

Anita Moorjani was another author I read that summer.

Her book *Dying to Be Me* tells her story of a near death experience which kept her in a coma for over thirty hours. Revelations during that period of time allowed her to come back to this physical realm we inhabit with a deep understanding of where and how we fit into a Universal whole.

"I believe that when we leave our physical bodies, our infinite selves are all connected. In the pure consciousness state, we're all One. Many people have felt this unity during intense spiritual experiences or out in nature. When we work with animals or have pets, we feel it, too. We sometimes experience synchronicity and even extrasensory perception (ESP) and other such phenomena as a result of our being One with all creation, but because most people aren't aware of it, it doesn't happen as often as it could.

In truth, I'm not my body, my race, religion, or other beliefs, and neither is anyone else. The real self is infinite and much more powerful a complete and whole entity that isn't broken or damaged in any way. The infinite me already contains all the resources I need to navigate through life, because I'm One with Universal energy. In fact, I am Universal energy."

~ Anita Moorjani from Dying To Be Me

During that summer of reading, I practiced the concepts these authors shared. I began allowing the Universe to give answers, expecting I would recognize and accept the messages being given if I just watched...listened! I found myself questioning my marriage, where we were living, and our financial choices.

"*What and where am I supposed to be?*" I stated my question and with a deep breath said, "Thank you Universe. Thank you for the guidance."

I am aware, I am receptive and I am accepting. My mantra was born.

These many years later, I recognize that this summer of 2011 was my first course in the lessons of gratitude. Gratitude in advance for those answers and circumstances desired. Gratitude with the complete and utter conviction that the answers we seek are there for us...already in play... and will show when we are ready to see them.

It was the summer I came to understand that the Universe will co-conspire on our behalf if we allow.

"The Universe is saying: Allow me to flow through you unrestricted, and you will see the greatest magic you have ever seen." ~ Klaus Joehle

It was the summer I deleted the concept of *coincidence* from my thought pattern and shifted my conscious awareness to recognizing synchronicities, and accepted that I was, in fact, being given answers and guidance. All I had to do was let the Universe *do its thing* and pay attention. It was whispering...my job was to listen!

While rummaging through a dusty bookshelf late in the summer I found a copy of Paulo Coelho's *The Pilgrimage* tucked between shelves and the wall, cobwebs disintegrating as I pulled it from hiding.

Soaking in his words a second time in two years, I was drawn to this Camino he spoke of—the Camino Santiago de Compostela. This famed pilgrimage path, trod for over a thousand years by pilgrims seeking to reach the burial place of St. James the Apostle in Santiago de Compostela, stretches 800 kilometers from St. Jean Pied du Port in the French Pyrenees to Santiago in Galician Spain. Haunting, his tale of this magical trek spoke to my soul. Energy pulling me toward this walk.

I recognized that finding Coelho's book again now, after several years in hiding, was a gift from the Universe. Trusting in the timing, the synchronicity of this, I knew in my soul I would walk.

Never in my life had I felt such an undeniable conviction that I was to do anything so immensely contrary to my nature. I was not an outdoorsy athletic type woman and certainly not someone who would choose the physical call to walk twelve to fifteen miles a day. Yet, I knew.

I knew I would walk the Camino just as hundreds of thousands of pilgrims over the centuries had done. Pilgrims before me had walked in penance, walked in search of a miracle to heal broken bodies, and walked seeking answers to troubled souls. That I would join them was now a given.

The when and how were not important...those answers would come. That I would walk was undeniable.

2012 New Year's Day in Rovinj

Huddled around a table for two, three local girlfriends joined me for cappuccino. We pulled chairs and made ourselves quite at home at a local cafe. Bundled in scarves and sweaters, we opted to sit outdoors soaking in rays of sun glinting through leftover morning clouds. Clouds; far too many clouds these last early winter months.

We took turns sharing our plans for the new year ahead.

"Well, the gallery will be ready in early May, maybe by my birthday" said Jan, local British artist and my dearest girlfriend here.

"Classes, students; it will be the same." Zuze made even this mundane statement sound joyful. I admired her energy.

"I am going to show my art in Holy Trinity Church; the octagonal one. I won the chance to use it as a gallery this year!" Jadranka is beside herself with excitement at having a gallery space.

My turn. "I am going to walk the Camino." All three stared at me with mouths agape.

"You're doing what?" they questioned in unison, excitement in their words.

"I am going to walk the Camino," I repeated, grinning broadly.

I heard the conviction in my own voice, felt again the energy pull of this walk. I was going to walk the Camino Santiago de Compostela and discover who and what I was to be in this life.

CHAPTER FOUR

MJ

"When angels visit us we do not hear the rustle of wings, nor feel the feathery breast of the dove; but we know their presence by the love they create in our hearts." ~ Mary Baker Eddy

I t had been eight months since I reread *The Pilgrimage* and knew I would walk the Camino; four months since I heard my voice announce confidently to my friends that I was going to walk. It was May of 2012—my birthday month.

During the past winter, Jack and I had been seriously reconsidering a move to Spain—Moraira to be exact. Having lived overseas for three and a half years, by this time we were more confident in our ability to obtain the appropriate visas.

Moraira. The village Jack and I fell in love with during a scouting expedition in January of 2008. Just a few months earlier, in November of 2007, he and his brother Mike and my son Greg, had spent two weeks scouring the Costa Blanca area for the perfect village. Of course, a great deal of internet searching had taken place prior to that journey: studying, reviewing, gleaning all the information we could as we weighed options and considered the overseas move we had decided upon. The Costa Blanca had been our choice.

In 2010, two years after moving to Rovinj, we had invested in an older apartment in the center of Moraira. After an extensive remodel, we joined up with a local vacation rental company and put it in their rental pool. Our hope was that this apartment would become our home one day. In a multicultural village, home to a multitude of English speaking expats from Holland, Germany, the UK, we had a much better match for a long-term social life in Europe.

We owned our apartment in Rovinj and had purchased a small holiday rental apartment I was managing. A way to keep busy, make a little income and, we had hoped, fit into the community better. Yet, after almost four years in an environment in which the majority of the locals, relatively fresh off a dictatorship prior to the 1990s war, seemed to question two Americans living full-time in their midst, we felt we were ready for a fresh start. Decision made. Logistics would be an issue, but we felt ready to make the move to the town that had held our hearts: Moraira on the Costa Blanca in Spain.

Both Rovinj apartments went on the market and the new home adventure began. With us, every four years seemed to be our turnaround for a new house, a new start. As I look back to our first home together and trace the sales and purchases since, paperwork would reveal we were underway on a new project almost to the month each time. We had become accustomed to the family ribbing.

"Hey guys; four years. Bought a new house yet? Isn't it time?"

What they didn't realize is that those four-year turnarounds had become part of an unconscious dance keeping a fragile marriage intact.

On the outside we looked picture perfect. We held successful hotel careers, both managing high-end boutique hotels at the time of our departure for the overseas dream. A gorgeous expansive view over a freshly-mowed lawn out to the sparkling blue waters of the Puget Sound greeted us from the living room each morning. Gardens teemed with the not-so-ordinary florals thanks to past owners with green thumbs. Our handsome, intelligent son was moving up quickly in his restaurant career, moving forward in his life. Three lovable doggies romped about the house. There was money to travel, family, friends. Our annual summer bash was anxiously awaited by friends and colleagues, past and present. Some seventy-five guests drank, dined, and danced the day away to our eclectic mix of German schlager (a tribute to the family's Bavarian heritage), disco, country, and the best of the 70s and 80s. We had worked hard for this life and were in the prime of our careers. It looked perfect.

Now after four years in Rovinj, again the 'move and do something new' bug had bit. Moving is an expensive undertaking. We had spent a small fortune making the overseas move from the United States to Rovinj. And it seemed like time again. It becomes even more expensive when considering the logistics of a household transfer from Croatia to Spain—a country outside the EU into a country within the EU. Rules and regulations made for some tricky juggling, and definitely an increase in costs.

Keep in mind, while all of this was going on, I was still committed and planning a pilgrimage walk that would take me away from home, wherever that was, for a solid six weeks. Time away and the costs incurred weighed heavily on my mind. Although a start date had not been set in stone, I was clear that sometime in the spring of 2013 would be my Camino. My research convinced me that April through late May was one of the most alluring seasons along the Camino Frances, the stretch I would walk. As far as I was concerned, I was just over a year out from an incredible undertaking, the likes of which I had never attempted, and less than a year to go with a major move slated for the fall.

Then one sloppy, wet gray morning, the email notification on our laptop pinged. I caught a quick peek at the screen as I breezed across our tiny living area. Sinister words crept silently across the subject line:

Mary Jo is very ill—she is going into the hospital.

Set the coffee cup down quickly...don't spill Kate...your hands are shaking...Deep breath...sit down...read slowly.

My Aunt Mary Jo, more big sister than Aunt as we were only four years apart in age, had fought multiples sclerosis for years. With MS, her body had lost its resistance, organs weakened over time, lungs no longer able to breathe fully. Pneumonia had set in again. This time it would win the battle. It was February. I purchased a ticket and flew home to Washington State.

Our friendship was rich and deep. I loved her dearly. We had been chosen friends for years.

Please let me make it in time. Please God let her know I am here.

When I reached the hospital, the nurses suggested I ask her to wiggle a toe if she heard me. The ventilator forcing air into weakened lungs was deafening in my ears.

"MJ? MJ, I'm here. It's Kate; I am right here." The slightest of wiggles greeted my words.

Two days later she died. Through the tears, the sadness and loss, I felt such overwhelming joy. She was free. Her spirit would become the Mary Jo, MJ, of her youth—young and healthy. She would run in spring flowered fields and race along the glistening sunset ocean beaches she loved. And I knew she would be with me. Sis taught me through her 11s over the years. MJ's spirit would whisper...all I had to do was listen.

Back in Rovinj several weeks later, and the move plans were well are underway. Fall was to be our timeframe. Five months. Feeling the pinch of finances, I reminded myself daily that everything had pointed to this move. Logistics were falling into place and we had an apartment we loved waiting for us in Moraira. There was no reason to doubt. Friends there were looking forward to having us in the village full-time. Overall, I felt completely assured that the move, along with being an exciting undertaking, was the *right* undertaking. And, Jack and I enjoyed the process.

I practiced all I had learned in the last few months since the summer. I remained focused on all that was good and right with our marriage and left the troubled areas aside. My one great fear in those last months before the move was the finances. I found the concern over mounting costs eating at me, waking me at night out of troubled dreams.

It was only spring, yet the Adriatic humidity took its toll on the body. One afternoon, drained from the heat, I lay down to rest under the cooling swish-swoosh of bedroom fan blades whirling above.

Focused on our dwindling reserve of cash, I lay perfectly still. Staring out the bedroom window, eyes focused on the bell tower of St. Francis church a half block down the narrow cobbled alleyway, my back faced our bedroom door.

A weight, firm, compressed the bed near the small of my back. Smiling, I reached behind me encouraging our sweet black lab Lucky to settle in for a nap.

"Come on Lucky. Cuddle here with me under the fan."

Patting the bed to welcome him up for a snooze, my hand brushed only air. No Lucky.

Again, a firm weight shifted at the small of my back. Startled I sat up, quickly turning to look, fingers grazing the bed where the weight settled.

"The money is in the bank. You will have it when you need it. It is there."

I immediately recognized her voice, her love. MJ. Her words, imprints on my heart, more a feeling than a voice. Words that wrapped my spirit in comfort. Her voice was that of reassurance. Calm. Quiet. It was as if she spoke directly in my head. Directly to my soul.

Mary Jo knew what I had been unable to trust. Her world was now multi-dimensional. Her spirit, her energy, flowed between past and present, here and there because all time and space are meshed as one. With my newfound acceptance of life as energy, always free flowing and connected, her presence seemed perfectly normal.

Would I have recognized this a year ago? Would I have accepted? Sis has been real to me for years but this is different.

Mary Jo spoke directly to my soul.

"The money is in the bank."

Quiet, peace...her presence faded away as quickly as she had come.

Tears of joy fell as I sat up laughing at the happiness of her visit.

There, on my bed, I connected to her energy, she to mine. Her words offered the security I desperately needed.

All would be well. Everything was in Divine order.

Our move to Spain was safe. I would walk my Camino.

CHAPTER FIVE

Visitations

"A cloud does not know why it moves in just such a direction and at such a speed...It feels an impulsion...this is the place to go now. But the sky knows the reasons and the patterns behind all clouds, and you will know, too, when you lift yourself high enough to see beyond horizons."

~ Richard Bach

By the summer of 2013, Jack and I were living in Moraira. Offers on our condo style apartment had eased my mind regarding finances. The move from Rovinj, with all of its challenges, had brought us to the picturesque Spanish pueblo on the shores of the Mediterranean that had held our hearts for years. Once again a new life was beginning, four years later as was our dance.

A wide circle of friends grew. A more limited social life in Rovinj was replaced with weekly Sunday lunch parties. Cocktails at a favorite German bar kept Jack speaking the language of his upbringing with a group of like-minded guys. He had been missing male camaraderie in Rovinj. This was perfect! We joined the U.S. Navy League, represented locally by expat Americans, Scottish, Dutch, and British. And always a gathering could be found at our favorite bar just down the main cobbled street.

The apartment we had rescued from its 1950s interior for use as a high quality rental was now cozy with our personal belongings. Our memories of nineteen years together surrounded us. It had become the European home we envisioned. Just enough room for us, our beloved black Lab, Lucky, and visitors when they came. Positioned in the heart of the pueblo, it was ideal for the life we dreamed of in Spain.

What was missing in this move however was that newfound spark; that *every-four-year boost* in excitement that the planning, purchase, and settling in always brought. On the outside we imitated the perfect expat life and were the envy of friends locally, as well as in the States. We looked ideal! Truthfully, we both knew. The walls, the structure of our marriage, were crumbling and would come crashing down.

Sea

The sea is my grounding, my connection to earth and soul. Whenever my spirit is weak...tired of trying to maneuver the challenges of life...the sea calms me and offers me a place of solace.

On a brilliant summer morning, my brain mired in the questions spinning regarding my faltering marriage, I escaped to the sea.

Could we go on without professional help? My two-year transition into a life of focusing on the positive to bring about change hasn't been enough—now what?

At the edge of the harbor park, I descended the narrow winding stone staircase toward the crystal blue Mediterranean. My favorite rock promontory, sequestered from village life, offered solitude. Offered peace. There above the lapping blue waters, below the noise of the road above, I knew I could escape into nothingness. *Breathe, Kate. Breathe...slowly.*

Air, rich with the scent of seaweed, filled my lungs as little by little angst dissolved. With eyes closed, my spinning muddled brain began to empty of all thought. My heart which fought to remain open, searching to stay positive, slowed its troubled beating. My mantra of the last two years replayed as I sat staring into the vast Mediterranean.

I am aware. I am receptive. I am accepting.

Minutes passed. Shrouded in moist sea air, I heard nothing. The questioning had stopped....my heart was calm.

Visions of drifting clouds floated across the horizon. Focused on whirls of white, I sank deeper and deeper into the center of this energy. Calm...purity...peace.

"Katy, Katy my love," my grandmother's voice whispered my name.

She had called me Katy from birth, a nickname to the elegant Katharine, my given name. Long passed away for over twenty years, the familiar timbre of her soft voice hugged me and drew me close to her heart. I had been her *Katy, my love* for as long as I knew.

A brief whiff of spicy applewood pipe tobacco encircled my senses.

Grandpa?

Breathing in deeply, inhaling the essence of his memory, I pulled him in. No words, yet the aroma of a flavored tobacco told me he was here, his pipe lit, his arms wide open to gather me in loving arms. My grandmother and grandfather, loving energy, from a plane somewhere beyond this world. We were connected completely.

Softly, once again I heard her loving voice.

"Katy, my love."

My grandfather's pipe tobacco swirled, and his arms lifted me onto a lap I knew would protect me.

In the same breath, a myriad of clouds flew across the sky. Soft billowing marshmallow puffs of cloud quickly became angry darkened masses. In the same moment, edging away at the darkened shadows, pink veils of translucence came filtering through the shadows. Clouds of peace crossing clouds of thunder. All drifting simultaneously before me in brilliant clarity.

"Everything happens at once, Kate. I can be everywhere at once. See, it all happens at the same time." Jeannie's voice bubbled with excitement as she shared what she now knew from her angel world.

No time differential existed as I sat fixated on the horizon. Clouds dancing in and out, circling, melding together and separating again as if to say, "See! She's right you know. Everything happens at once. No past or present, here or there—everything is *now*."

Once, just after Mary Jo died, Jeannie had come to me in a dream. Actually, I believe it was a visit. Dreams versus visits from those we have lost; there is a distinct difference. As the vision of what she shared played over and over in my mind, I accepted that she had in fact come to show me what she had learned since her death five years earlier. It was early 2012 and by that time, I knew enough to accept angels sharing their wisdom.

The vision: butter yellow cake batter in a large, old fashioned Corning Ware mixing bowl. Blue with white scrolling design work. A handheld electric mixer, operating solely on its own accord, whipped the batter creamy smooth. As I lifted the bowl, pouring the batter into a waiting cake tin, the batter slowly disappeared. It was there—it was gone. Holding an empty bowl over a waiting pan, the cascading batter simply vanished.

Confused, I put the bowl on the counter and lifted the mixer holding it poised over the bowl. Suddenly, the bowl was again filled with batter. It had reappeared. In that moment Jeannie's voice, a voice I had not heard in five years since her death, spoke clearly:

"Just because you don't see it, doesn't mean it isn't there."

And then it was over.

It took no time at all for me to realize the truth of what she shared that day. Her visit validated what I had been reading; what I clumsily practiced in setting my intentions and allowing myself to attempt co-conspiring with the Universe. With every fiber of my being, I believe that this physical world we live in, this world we call home, is but a fraction of the multi-dimensional Universe at play...a matrix of energy...interconnected on every level.

Just because I don't see it doesn't mean it isn't there.

A seagull's caw jolted me back. Motors in passing cars on the roadway above slowed as they rounded the bend, the incredible sea views of Moraira prompting drivers to pause somewhere high above my secret portal in time. Time stood still; suspended. *How long had I been here?*

Quietly contemplating the voices, the visions of the last hour, one thought became perfectly clear. I had been blessed with an undeniable visit from my grandparents and my sister, all passed away long ago. I had been reminded that I am intrinsically connected to Universal love. The spirits of those who have left us are, in fact, here with us. They are here with us and *they are love*. In rare moments when we totally open our hearts and souls to accepting their communication, we can be reached...touched. And I had been blessed.

Surrender. The morning's tapestry of contrasting clouds, each signaling a truth of existence...coexisting in the same space...allowed the flow of nature to simply take its course. I witnessed a show of grace and simplicity in surrender. *Surrender to what is—accept life as it is, not as I think it should be.*

That serene morning in the summer of 2013, I chose to surrender. Accept my marriage as it was.

Surrendering and giving up are not the same. To surrender allows the flow of the Universe without fighting what is. Surrender is allowing. Giving up is to quit trying, to admit defeat.

My decision: surrender to the energies of the Universe. If this marriage was to be...if it was meant to exist as a whole and healthy union...Jack will step forward and take part in the healing. I am to love him. Be kind, be loving, choose grace.

And, I will prepare to walk my Camino as I know in my soul I am meant to.

CHAPTER SIX

Crossroads

"Allow whatever you feel deep within you in that quiet and peaceful space to guide you in a direction that is your true destiny." ~ Dr. Wayne Dyer

I believe Jack saw a change in me as I grew solid in myself again. I became calm, focused, intent on seeing the positive in all circumstances. Steadfast in my renewed belief that the Universe shows us the truths we need to learn at the precise time and place we need them, the miraculous connection I felt...the lessons taught...that summer morning of 2013 on the promontory above the sea carried me for months. With a feeling of love and a belief that our marriage would evolve as it was meant, I focused on my Camino.

During the next months of daily walking, preparing for this 800-plus km adventure by adding distance and altitude little by little, my Camino was becoming a reality. Friends joined me, three in particular, and in doing so found themselves drawn to the calling of this Camino: Camino de Santiago. In the end, two of them would be with me at various times during the walk.

Dedicated to keeping our marriage together, I invited Jack to join me on the Camino. I invited him many mornings to come train with me. His coming on this Camino would bring forth a much different experience than the one I had read so much about...the experience which called to my soul. But he was my husband and perhaps, just perhaps, sharing such an experience as the Camino would provide a new bond...a new spark.

I imagine that just as when any one person in a union begins to grow, and the flow of the relationship dance changes, Jack felt the rhythm of our marriage shift. Yet, he did not join. He remained emotionally removed...uninvolved. All of my '*law of attraction...practice gratitude*' positivity was not going to change him. It was not supposed to change him.

But I was definitely changing. I was becoming strong and healthy: emotionally, physically, and spiritually. Jack was content as he was. He opted for the status quo.

It is no wonder that by the spring of 2014 when he finally spoke his truth, a truth I believe he had held inside for years, divorce was his recommendation. My request for counseling, or at least some self-help reading together, was not an option for him.

With his announcement that we were to be divorced, I spent the summer in the States focused on my upcoming Camino, trying to determine who and what life would bring. Conversations between us over the next couple of months went from the briefest hope of healing to angry emails.

By the time I returned to Spain a few days before beginning the adventure of the Camino in September, we were civil. We were able to be in each other's company relatively comfortably over the ten days before I left to walk. We shared laughter and a quick hug now and again...and a tearful kiss goodbye. Perhaps, just perhaps, there was hope?

El Camino de Santiago

My Camino Prayer

Because I believe the Universe conspires on our behalf...because I believe angels are actively involved in our daily life and offer amazing insight if we listen and watch...because I believe in the beauty of each day and know we have the opportunity to choose our thoughts and state of mind...I see this glorious day begin to unfold and know in my soul these travels will be safe, inspiring, a chance once again, to behold the magnificence of this planet we call home...and I feel blessed.

CHAPTER SEVEN

Camino!

"Listen to your heart. It knows everything."
~ Paulo Coelho

September 15th arrived! My backpack was loaded, rearranged, adjusted, and checked again. It sat on the couch of a friend's apartment anxiously waiting to settle in on my back. From here on out we would be one, my backpack and I!

Talismans from friends and family adorned the straps and cords. Guardian angels from Mom and my sister Mary. The traditional scallop shell, symbol of the Camino, a gift from my brother-in-law, hung square in the center, leather cord tied snug. A Swarovski jeweled gecko from my dear girlfriend Beverly (every trekker girl needs a touch of bling) was front and center. And the blue and green colors of my hometown football team, the Seattle Seahawks, from life friend and fellow football fanatic, Fawn, hung on a side pocket. Not exactly your quiet unassuming pack, mine screamed "I am here and I am loved...and, OH by the way, I believe in good luck charms!"

Liz's hubby drove her into town to meet me on this brilliant Mediterranean morning. Our plan: drive a rental car the eight hours from Moraira to San Sebastian in northern Spain. From there a train will whisk us into Bayonne, France and then on to St. Jean Pied de Port, traditional starting point for the Camino Frances. This is where we would begin our actual walk in two days.

Jack and Lucky wandered over from our, his, apartment a couple blocks away to see us off.

As we waited for Liz to arrive, Jack, bless him, reviewed safety issues, concerns, and cautions.... just as he had with each trip I had taken for the twenty years we had been together. It was a part of his love language. That he was still offering directions and advice warmed my heart.

And then she arrived and we were off!

The morning sun shone warm as Liz and I walked down the middle of a quiet Moraira street toward our rental car. Lucky trotted behind us determined to come along. I found myself wishing I knew what Jack was thinking and feeling at that moment. *But, have I ever really known? Has he ever been truly one hundred percent emotionally open? Was he capable?*

Years in the making, this trek was finally beginning. *Will it bring the clarity and sense of life purpose I have so been craving and searching to find in these last few months? My soul has known I would walk...I must trust the answers will come.*

Giddy with excitement, Liz and I laughed and sang the entire eight-hour drive. The countryside was breathtaking. Jack and I had driven much of this area before, but this time colors were more vibrant; river valleys and table top plateaus appeared wondrous in their creation. Perhaps because I knew I was about to walk land such as I witnessed on the drive, or perhaps because my whole being now saw all of life as a gift to be admired and treasured, the scenery took my breath away.

What I knew to be true is that the Camino my soul had drawn me toward was now beginning, and whatever wondrous truths I was to learn lay just ahead in the next few weeks.

I was elated!

CHAPTER EIGHT

Orisson

"We only notice 'signs' when they resonate a deep truth within. 'Signs' confirm the inner conviction that is too frightened to take action beyond those thoughts." ~ Annie Zalezsak

E ight kilometers from St. Jean Pied de Port to Orisson. Eight kilometers—a third of what we would walk most days. This was Day One on the Camino Frances, our route to Santiago. This route will cover 800 kilometers before we reach Santiago de Compostela. Many pilgrims will walk the twenty-four kilometer stretch across the Pyrenees to Roncesvalles in Spain on their first day. For Liz and I, Orisson at the end of a four-hour climb, would be far enough.

What I had learned through hours of blog reading and Camino preparatory homework was DO NOT OVERDO during the first days. Others who have made this journey make it clear: take it easy...this is not a race! I listened to that advice and opted to book two beds at the hostel in Orisson. In fact, I had booked them back in May!

The long slow climb felt, on this first day, as if it were ten vertical miles. We climbed, lungs fighting for air...stopping...leaning on our sticks while pulses slow...then started again. Our new walking sticks, purchased from a local vendor in St. Jean the evening before, tapped a slow rhythm as we progressed. A few other pilgrims opted to trudge beaten paths through hillside fields. They crossed our road now and again, as the road route we walked had switchback turns to ease the ascent. As their paths crossed ours we jubilantly wish each other a warm "Buen Camino!" and went on our way. Quiet tapping of our sticks on the asphalt, paths crisscrossing the road to Orisson, lulled me to memories of when I feared this Camino may not happen.

Andalusia

Jack and I were driving a main highway through Andalusian Spain in the summer of 2013. Olive groves stretched to the horizon and beyond, evening light shimmering with the heat of the late afternoon. A long weekend away had been filled with love and laughter. Jack and Kate, the best of friends, seeing new sights, experiencing more of this Spanish country we had come to call home. Were we healing?

Perhaps because our marriage had become more serene, I found my conscience tugging. *Should I still go? If I invite him, it will not be the Camino my soul has called me to walk. He will drink. He will sleep later in the mornings. He will not want to stay at pilgrim albergues and hostels, a part of the experience I am so anxious to be a part of. Do I go without him? Do I set the dream aside? And, has he really shown any interest in joining?*

The speed limit was seventy kilometers per hour. We were not crawling along by any means. As conflict jostled my emotions, just to the right out of my side passenger window, I caught a glimpse of a gravel pathway, a path meandering through the olive groves ending just alongside the highway. Bright in the evening Spanish sun, a sign I had come to recognize yet had never seen before except on the internet and in books, crossed my field of vision—a daffodil yellow scallop shell rising against a brilliant blue background, attached to a signpost at the meeting of trail and road. This was the way marker for the Camino de Santiago...the signage for pilgrims following the paths to Santiago de Compostela! There, in southern Spain, a path and a scallop shell called out to me at the precise time I questioned whether I stay or go. Incredible!

I realized immediately that a gift from the Universe had been given, precisely when I needed it most. Smiling, my mind relaxed, I caught a glimpse of the dashboard clock. It read 7:11.

Sis, once again from her realm beyond, letting me know all was well, reaffirming. Everything is in order. I *will* walk my Camino.

Listen to the whispers...the answers are all around.

Tap...tap...tap...the rhythmic sound of pole tips to road brought me back. Pilgrims crossed the road ahead from shortcuts across the fields.

The road to Santiago...my road.

CHAPTER NINE

A Camino Family is Born

"An invisible thread connects those who are destined to meet, regardless of time, place or circumstance. The thread may stretch or tangle, but will never break." ~ Chinese legend

"Ladies, come join us"!

They called to us in English. American English. We had spent the morning on the climb to Orisson hearing British and Australian versions. For the first time that day we heard Americans.

Two men, sixty somethings. Their demeanor told me they were dear and true friends, completely ecstatic to be sitting on the outdoor terrace of this *refuge* at Orisson.

"We have smoked salmon. Bring your beers and come sit!"

Their voices were filled with enthusiasm. Infectious!

Liz and I gathered the well-earned iced mugs of beer we were sipping, pulled our weary bodies from where we flopped down earlier, and wandered over to their table across the immense outdoor terrace. Two fellow Americans, promising a feast, were gathering pilgrims on this first day.

"Pacific Northwest salmon," they announced proudly.

A flurry of questions arose from others trying to picture where the Pacific Northwest might fit on a map. Pilgrims from a variety of European nations, many unfamiliar with the expanse of the United States, began a stream of questions.

"I have a cousin in California. Is it near there?" asked one pellegrina.

"My sister lives in Denver. I don't think that's close, is it?" questioned a man from Holland.

"Pacific Northwest?" I asked with surprise. "What city?"

"Seattle area," they answered in unison.

"Richmond Beach to be exact," said one, smiling.

I am sure my mouth fell open in an astonished gape. Jack and I left that exact same neighborhood when we moved overseas six years earlier. Our house, near Richmond Beach, had been our dream home. Gardens, an expansive lawn, and a view of the Olympic Mountains across the waters of Puget Sound. Four years later, after watching Jack's mom and my middle sister die within months of each other, this had been the house we ran from before our marriage, too, might die.

Six years and there in the Pyrenees mountains of southern France, the first pilgrims we connected with were from this same neighborhood. *Universe, what's going on?*

The afternoon flew by as fellow travelers were shown to their beds, or tents in some cases. As some left, more joined. These two guys had created a party! And then we learned they had done this before.

They had walked this Camino just the year before and had enjoyed the time of their lives. Now, two lifelong buddies were following their hearts, walking the pilgrimage again, beginning on the exact same date.

Their first night in Orisson had been one of the greatest memories of their adventure and they were determined to recreate and offer that sense of camaraderie and excitement to us newbies. It worked! By 4 p.m., there must have been twenty of us laughing, sharing information on hometowns, our Camino hopes and dreams for the next few weeks, and promises to keep an eye out for each other along the way. Pacific Northwest smoked salmon, beer and wine—a Camino family was born!

Liz and I got the nod from the *hosteliero* to follow her to our beds. Our first night out and we were to learn what pilgrim life would entail when sharing space with strangers. Juggling time and tight spaces to get a turn in limited shower facilities, finding open space in the sun on the communal clothesline and hoping, by all hopes, that a bathroom was available when needed!

Checked into our shared bunk bed room, a room for only six, Liz and I laughed as Paul and Guy, our Pacific Northwest smoked salmon buddies, turned to greet us from their already claimed beds.

"Girls; how perfect! We couldn't have asked for any better roommates."

CHAPTER TEN

Soar

"Surrender=Complete acceptance of what is +
Faith that all is well, even without my input."
~ Dr. Amy Johnson

Believing as I do that there are no coincidences in life, it came as no surprise when, the next morning as we stumbled down to breakfast, Paul and Guy ushered us to their table just inside the door and explained the breakfast process. Stacks of small soup bowls sat next to steaming coffee urns. Recognizing our bewilderment, the guys handed us each a bowl and demonstrated the Navarra tradition of drinking coffee from a soup bowl. A quick glance around the packed dining hall told me they were not pulling our legs—this is how it was done. Think sipping one's sweet and sour soup from a bowl—same difference. The coffee was dark and rich; it tasted heavenly!

Breakfast consisted of thick toasted *pan,* home churned butter the color of marigolds, and a berry jam only a practiced *abuela* could make. A divine start to Day Two.

"Well ladies, shall we walk together?"

Liz and I smiled and accepted with glee. These two struck us as genuinely good men. Kind, intelligent and, after yesterday's afternoon terrace party, we knew without a doubt a hell of a lot of fun!

Backpacks on, walking sticks in hand, we marched into the pre-dawn glow of light.

The warm winds blew us sideways as we made our way from Orisson, in France to Roncesvalle, our first stop on the Spanish side of the Pyrenees. I am not a small woman. Six feet in height with the bone structure of my Cherokee and German forefathers, I fought to stay grounded as we passed verdant green hillsides, sheep gathered in tight flocks staving off the winds.

The walk took us sixteen kilometers, and again, much of the trek was an uphill slope, although not as intense as the day before. We stopped to rest, feet spread apart, firmly planted creating a solid base. Fifty-kilometer-per-hour gusts buffeted our backpacks, threatening to lift our walking sticks from the path.

Grounded; a thought-provoking word. Once upon a time I had felt grounded. A relationship with a man I loved, a career, fulfilling, successful. Drinking had always been the fluttering red flag somewhere in the distance. Drinking loosened him, allowed him to release the hurt and stress, brought forth the fun Jack. And I, in desperate need of spontaneity and joy in my life, had joined in the party. It is who we were.

Not that drinking was all we did, and certainly it did not impinge on stellar careers, but it defined our social life. It defined weekends: Bloody Marys on a Sunday morning, Saturday afternoons at the local pub sipping beers while he slowly let down his guard and really talked...shared himself with me. I relished those days.

Did I encourage these times? I did. Eyes closed, refusing to contemplate the full picture of what I was helping to create.

When had I come to see that fluttering flag? When had I fully recognized and accepted this warning sign as real, signaling the potential storms?

I simply lowered my head and marched through, just as I fought my way through the gales on the road to Ronces-valles. Focused on where I wanted to be, I refused to look around me. I refused to recognize the signs.

A cheer erupted from Paul and Guy as we reached an immense boulder alongside the path we were traveling. Once again, I was pulled into the present from somewhere deep within myself.

Warm winds whipping arms and legs, we had reached the highest point in our climb across the Pyrenees! Bags dropped unceremoniously as one by one we climbed the rock stage, raised walking sticks and poles high into the air, fighting to stay standing, and shot photos commemorating our achievement. Liz and me, Liz and the guys, me and the guys. You would think we discovered a new land! Joyfully, we claimed this moment in time.

The remainder of our walk that day raced by as we traversed wooded glens, past historical markers honoring pilgrims who had walked this path before us. Finally, we worked our way along the steep descent into Roncesvalles.

Swooping from high overhead, a majestic condor dove toward us. Staring deep into endless blue sky, we watched, riveted, as one amazing bird became two, two became four, all sharing in the joyful play of riding the updrafts from the valley below.

Their wingspans must have stretched six feet wide as they quietly, slowly, caught the air and glided. Present. They were present in the moment...just floating...instinctively knowing they were safe.

The Universe whispers in the most remarkable ways. And the Camino teaches. Aware I could trudge against the gales, against the challenges of facing a dead marriage, with my head down, or I could let go.

I could surrender and in doing so catch the updraft of Universal energy and *soar*! On the hillside above Roncesvalles, in the shadow of gliding condor wings, I choose surrender...surrender and *soar*!

CHAPTER ELEVEN

Gratitude

*"Gratitude bestows reverence allowing us to en-
counter everyday epiphanies, those transcendent
moments of awe that change forever how we experience life and the world."*
~ *John Milton*

A t some point in this journey of discovering the energies of the Universe, the connectedness I learned ex-
ists if I only listen, I came across the book *The Magic* by
Rhonda Byrne.

As with *The Secret*, well renowned for sharing the concept of the *law of attraction* with the world, *The Magic*
speaks to the importance of recognizing gratitude as a way
of attracting more into our lives. We can bring more love,
more security, more financial reward...more of what we

practice being grateful in receiving. Give sincere thanks, in advance, for all you have and desire and more of the same flows into your life. *Like attracts like.*

Taking this idea to heart, gratitude...conscious gratitude...became part of my daily world. It may sound a tad simplistic, but even the smallest things: a parking place coming available right as I neared it, finding a sale on just the item I needed but felt too expensive, these became moments to say "Thank you Universe."

What happened, of course, is that I began to fully comprehend, realized, how many gifts are given to me each and every day. And the more I said "thank you," the more those gifts multiplied.

By the beginning of my Camino, expressing gratitude throughout the day was an integral part of my belief. What I also found was that the more I practiced gratitude, the more aware I became of other people and their expressions of gratitude. A domino effect of "thank yous."

Zubiri

The morning we walked out of Zubiri felt extraordinarily long. By 11 a.m., with no cafes in sight, it was clear that the snacks we purchased in a local *tienda* the evening before were going to be much needed. Between the four of us we had almonds, oranges, crackers, apples, a banana, and dark chocolate. We *always* had dark chocolate! It was a mid-morning feast as we perched on a craggy ledge along a village wall.

An elderly Korean woman walked into the plaza where we were sitting. She carried her large backpack with the waist strap uncinched. I think that is what caught our attention. She looked uncomfortable. The weight, carried completely on her shoulders, must have caused pain. She was small in height, yet stocky and strong in her build. She came upon us as we rested and snacked. I am not sure how we knew she was without a bite to eat or that her water had run low; we just did. We recognized her discomfort. And, as pilgrims do, we offered to share our feast, which she gracefully turned down.

A bit of coaxing though and we convinced her it was perfectly okay, we had plenty, and isn't sharing the camaraderie of the Camino after all? She acquiesced, happily accepting segments of a juicy sweet orange, munching almonds and crackers, and savoring the sweet dark chocolate. She chatted ever so briefly and was off, backpack weighing heavy over her shoulders. I found myself wondering what emotional burdens she may be carrying. Why was she choosing to walk this pilgrimage alone at her age?

The next day, walking through a magnificent glade of woods, we came upon her resting against a tree. Excited to see us, she jumped to her feet and after the perfunctory "Buen Camino!" greeting, she offered each of us a share of her salty potato chips.

"Salt is important on this walk," she advised in broken English.

As she passed the sack to each of us, she bowed deeply,

person to person, *sincerely* thanking each for the portion of the mid-day snack they had provided the previous day.

"For the orange," to me; "For the almonds," to Guy; "For the crackers," to Paul; and "For the chocolate," to Liz.

That she could recall exactly which stranger had shared which food astonished me. Her warmth, simple depth of emotion, touched my heart.

Conscious gratitude takes work. It is almost an *art*. This pilgrim angel reminded me in the most vivid way of what is most important: our 'thank yous' must be clearly stated with honest emotion for the magic to work. This lovely Korean woman's detailed gratitude was a timely reminder of the importance of specificity and emotion in practicing gratitude.

My Rock

As the days rolled on, one into another, I found myself reliving the last few months leading to this Camino. I observed an amazing truth: over time I had been able to say thank you, with all sincerity, for the troubles in our marriage. I saw the patterns in the dance Jack and I shared for twenty years. My feelings of hurt were being set aside. Heart pains were replaced with a deeper sense of love....a love born of the knowledge that all aspects of our time together had their place in the path of my life and, without those times, I would not have learned the lessons intended. Someone once said, "Nothing in my life happens out of order." Now, I understood.

One of the practices recommended in Rhonda Byrne's *The Magic* is that of holding a small rock in the palm of your hand as you settle into sleep. This rock is your gratitude rock. With your gratitude rock in hand, recall the best thing that happened during that day. In searching for the best, the many gifts of the day are recounted and sleep comes while focused on positive thoughts. As science has proven time and again, the thoughts we carry into our slumber stay with us in our subconscious as we sleep, giving that much more time for our minds and bodies to absorb positive energies. The process intrigued me and I began the practice.

As my Camino got underway nine months later, my gratitude rock had been my bedside companion each night. A small speckled grey rock, it fit snug in my palm. Chosen as the waves washed the beach of Moraira, this rock had become an anchor. The physical touch brought to mind the gifts of the day. I often woke in the middle of the night, rock clutched tightly in my fist, and found myself smiling as I dozed off again, grateful. As a token of gratitude to the Universe, I decided I would lay down my rock at Cruz de Ferro, the Cross of Iron, when we reached this highest point of the Camino.

Clouded in mystery as to its true origins, some believe Cruz de Ferro was an altar erected to the Roman god Mercury. Others believe it was a worship site for the ancient Celts making their way through these Spanish lands. It is thought to have been Christianized in the eleventh century by Gaucelmo, founder of the Christian church at Foncebadon, the nearest village. Centuries later, it remains a sacred site for modern day pilgrims. For me it will be a place of surrender...of release.

Tradition says: Bring a rock from your homeland and lay the stone at the foot of the cross. A symbol of a pilgrim's personal troubles...burdens...the laying down of the stone symbolizes the release of that angst or worry. It is meant to be left behind. On to Santiago in a state of joy!

My plan: when I arrive at Cruz de Ferro, I will place my gratitude rock as a symbol of release. This is where I will lay down any last feelings of blame and hurt at a marriage ended. This is where I will commit again to focus, forever, on gratitude for the years of love and lessons Jack and I shared. I am ready. Nothing in my life has happened out of order. Thank you!

CHAPTER TWELVE

Jeannie

"Make yourself familiar with the angels and behold them frequently in spirit. For without being seen they are present with you." ~ St. Frances de Sale

On the morning of the sixth day, we walked up and out of Pamplona. The day brought a climb high above the elevated plateau of Pamplona and the surrounding valleys I had traversed this past week.

A warm fall mist glistened on mountains of haystacks...hay stacked so high four pilgrims could stand foot on shoulder, foot on shoulder, before reaching the top. Brilliantly colored hot air balloons floated above vast stretches of newly harvested fields. It was September. The misty air smelled of ripened grasses. Rich, dark dirt; minerals, wet, moist earth.

Ahead, on the highest hill I ascended that morning, wind turbines churned...long angular arms spinning, reaching, stretching high into the heavens. The gravel path stretched before me to the edge of the horizon. Step after step, three hours focused on the ground beneath my boots, ground worn down by the plodding feet of hundreds of thousands of pilgrims before me. My eyes focused on the turbines in the distance. They were my goal; their energy pulling me through.

I was intensely cognizant of country life around me. Songbirds whistled...a stray cat darted across the field in search of breakfast...farm dogs barked, sharing their stories, somewhere far beyond my sight. Shivers tickled my arms as the breeze on this hazy autumn morning brushed against my skin. My unsettled soul on edge.

What am I to do with my life? A marriage of twenty years is over. What purpose will unfold on this trek? Isn't that why I am here? Five days of walking...or has it been two weeks? Hour upon hour of thinking...remembering. Moments of laughter...moments of tears...all run together as I await my Camino answers. I trust in the Universe showing me. I am listening. Where is that calm serene knowing that will settle my soul?

Her voice came, warm, soft caresses around my heart. Jeannie's voice. It embraced me as a feeling...not words...yet, I heard her. I *heard* my Jeannie. Pancreatic cancer stole her away in the blink of an eye. Four months from diagnosis to death. Her voice was familiar, clear, speaking words directly into my heart...words flowing through my veins...my blood.

"Start writing. Don't ask what or why. Just start."

I stopped dead still in the center of the path, mesmerized...hearing her voice in me. *Where is she?* Turning to look behind me I saw only fields, the vast expanse of the plateau.

Her message was concise, yet offered in warmth and love. She spoke an order from beyond.

"Start writing."

I was not to question.

"Just start."

Her words reached deep, touched my soul and I knew, in that moment, what I was meant to do with the next chapter of my life. I had no idea why, yet I trusted in what she said. I knew without doubt that her words came from energies far beyond my limited scope...that she spoke my truth...my purpose.

"Start writing. Don't ask what or why...just start."

Jeannie, the energy of the Universe, once again brought answers to my listening soul. And how do I even explain this connection...this knowing...without the story of Jeannie?

Amazingly funny, full of sparkle; Jeannie, my middle sister, living life to the fullest. Never one to turn her back on a good time. Jeannie, hopping on an exquisite marble counter in a posh Maui hotel ladies room.... play surfing in the mirror. Knees bent holding the stance, her arms outstretched in balance mode...her visor wet from a last afternoon dunk in the hotel pool. A bubble gum pink swim cover-up drips as she plants her feet firmly in place and gives a final surfer pose, resplendent in style.

Jeannie, parked seductively on a bar stool at a beachside restaurant on Oahu, tanned and gorgeous, smiling at all the men, giving her "come get me" smile. Jeannie, sashaying to the ladies room, knowing how to turn the eyes. How I envied her innate ability to control a room, captivate an audience. Her 5'8" body, thin, limited curves, yet all female; she steals the looks away from every other woman in the bar, all eyes on her long brunette mane tumbling down her back. Her eyes glinting, a multicolored strapless sundress snug against her svelte frame, hips swinging ever so slightly as she makes her way across the floor. She is simply brilliant.

Jeannie, dancing in the dusk on the Honolulu beach. Warm rains are slowing, tapping the waves. In she goes. We have been told there are sharks after an early evening rain. No worries. Daredevil Jeannie, tee shirt hanging off a shoulder glinting bronze in the brief rays of sun through emerging blue skies, splashing, jumping, as the waves lap against her tanned legs. She calls me in to play in the waves, she and I the only two on the beach, running into the surf...into the sharks...splashing happily as rain, waves, sand tumble us to the shore...over and over we chase the odds and dodge the hidden dangers.

My sweet, beautiful Jeannie, now lying small, eaten away by cancer; cancer with its fingers huge and wide squeezing the life from her insides...cancer oozing through her organs, poisoning her every cell. Her body is shriveled, yet still fighting...fighting to remain in control...pain-killing drugs take over where alcohol left off. A brain not cooperating...her words are few...frightened...fighting for control. Fighting to stave off the death man coming to claim her from this world.

Why? Why take her? Why strip the vibrant spirit of this woman from this world? Penance. Does God really do this? Karma. Karma for past choices made...children hurt...family wounded? Chance. Does the Universe simply operate by chance?

I am with her the last twelve days. Hospice provides morphine, easing the excruciating pain. She reaches out and takes my arm with weakened fingers, no focus, her eyes open...vacant. She knows I am here. Her voice...a quiet whisper I barely hear.

"Katy, I love you."

Her thank you...her goodbye to me. Slipping deep under the ethers, she will soon leave.

"Katy, I love you."

Words I will carry always.

Jeannie, quiet, serene...she leaves her withered body...her final breath soft...her hands curled, childlike, under her cheeks. A last movement...she smiles so gently...a smile of joy...What has she seen? What does she now know?

The cancer is gone. Her tiny, once magnificent, svelte body lays quiet. Jeannie, her spirit, her soul, now soaring into the boundless endless stretches of the Universe...free...surfing once again...running in the waves...splashing...laughing...thick, sun-drenched brunette curls flowing as she dances in the light of the angels she joins.

On the ancient trail of the Camino the spirit of my Jeannie—her soul at one with the Universe—reached me. Wrapping me close, whispering the knowledge I had been seeking, she guides.

She came as angel wings, a gentle breeze bringing shivers in the late morning sun. My search for purpose, the search which led me to this trek of 500 miles, was being answered in her loving order to me:

"Start writing. Don't ask what or why...just start."

CHAPTER THIRTEEN

Reflections on the Meseta

"Every blade of grass has its angel that bends over it and whispers, 'Grow, grow.'"
~ The Talmud

Meseta: the Spanish term for a plateau or tabletop. The Northern meseta is a swath of flatland 150 kilometers across north central Spain. The portion we walked along the Camino Frances is at the northern edge, south of the Cantabrian Mountains, bordered on the east by the medieval city of Burgos and stretching west to Leon and Astorga, noble cities of the middle ages. This is farmland country. Rich verdant fields during the growing season disintegrate to dry, arid tracts of land in the scorching summer months.

As I walked in October 2014, freshly-turned fields

stretched as far as the naked eye could see. Drooping burnished gold heads languish atop six-foot-tall sunflower stalks. Once brilliant hues of sunbeam yellow, in the fall they are tired, withered, awaiting the harvesting combines which will pluck away their seeded faces for use as sunflower oil. An army of stalks marched across the meseta of Castilla-Leon at our side. Companions: morning, noon, and night.

For many pilgrims, this stretch of the Camino is perhaps the most challenging. No rugged ascents, no creeks to forge, simply mile upon mile of flattened landscape. Tedious monotony. Many hop a bus to Leon and bypass their boredom. Somewhere on the horizon, days ahead on winding trails, mountains peak through the floating clouds. On the early fall meseta we walked; dust, flies, fields freshly-turned and manured. Reasons to leave.

Villages sit camouflaged in gritty grey-ness atop slight elevations. They perch, watching over lands once nobly ruled. Ancient cracked buildings were now occupied primarily by the elderly. The young abandoned the land to the larger Spanish cities of the Castile-Leon region: Burgos, Astorga, Sahagun, Carrion and Leon itself, the magnificent once central city for all of northern Spain.

For me the northern meseta was one of the most incredible sections of this 800-kilometer walk. Reminiscent of my homeland in eastern Washington State, I felt calm, a connection to the wholeness of the Universe while on this land.

Six a.m. I led our group in the early morning hours.

Moving ahead under the glow of my headlamp, I quickened my step to gain distance from any veil of light tossed by the local village. I forged ahead of my fellow walkers as I moved into my private time.

On most meseta mornings, I switched off my headlamp about thirty minutes into our six to seven-hour walk. Standing motionless, staring into the vastness of space, I gazed as stars illuminated pre-dawn skies. A canopy of bright white light twinkled from horizon to horizon.

The Milky Way: eternal; resplendent. A tapestry of galaxies light years away lifted me up, holding me in a warm embrace. It was these early morning moments on the vast expanse of the meseta in which I was completely connected to all of time and space. Glittering stars danced bright in the sky. They shot across the heavens lighting the way, begging me to surrender and follow. On these five mornings as we crossed the openness of the Spanish meseta, I found myself contemplating the last three years of my life and the new transition in my thinking. It was a time of perfect reflection.

Breathe deep and leave the physical world behind— breathe in the consciousness of the Universe.

I believe I have always tried to live a kind life, a giving life. The biblical rule: "Do unto others as you would have them do unto you" has been a part of my upbringing. Perhaps not in an active church-going religion type of way, but certainly in the values my mother instilled as we were raised.

A precursor to a modern day *law of attraction,* the golden rule taught me the value of connecting with my fellow human beings, the importance of treating people, animals, all life, as valuable and worthy of love.

Is it not simply going a step further to understand that when we operate in the giving of ourselves, when we love because it is the *right* way to be, we are operating within the basic framework of the *law of attraction*? *The energy we put forth brings back to us like energy.*

Like attracts like.

Why then did it take me until that Rovinj summer of 2011 to carry this basic premise to the obvious next level, to put forth an energy of love, acceptance and faith in what will be and *expect* the same to return? It makes sense.

Co-conspire with the Universe. Surrender in faith and allow the Universe to work in my favor. I knew by now that this *allowing* was the answer. I had seen it in action! Undeniable messages from my mother-in-law Sis using her :11 communication connection. A Camino road sign in the southern interior of Spain just as I was trying to decide whether to attempt the pilgrimage I felt compelled to walk. I had surrendered on a mystical summer day a year ago, one brilliant morning on a rocky promontory in Moraira. Without question I was one with the magnificence of the Universe. My sister, my grandparents, they had spoken to me as clearly as if they sat alongside me as I gazed at the sea. A sea blanketed with clouds transforming from billowing cotton candy masses to thunderstorm boulders in the sky, all in a matter of moments.

That morning I had recognized that to *allow* was all I could do in my marriage. And, in that surrender, that acceptance of Jack as the man he was and knowing I could expect no more, the next few months of our lives would lead us to a final break, would lead us to begin the new lives which had been waiting all along. For me, the break would lead to a Camino exactly as my soul had known it was meant to be—joyous, reflective, healthy—a full experience of the being.

The lessons of the summer of 2011 in Rovinj had spiraled me into a learning curve. Three years of momentum as I came to believe and understand what is available to us if we are

Aware—Receptive—Accepting.

Surrendering concerns and angst to the Universe, allowing a free-flowing energy connection, was step one for me.

* * *

"In the attitude of silence the soul finds the path in a clearer light, and what is elusive and deceptive resolves itself into crystal clearness. Our life is a long and arduous quest after Truth."
~ Mahatma Gandhi

Step Two had become the practice of meditation. It became clear that if I was going to surrender my problems, I had better learn to be in the correct state of mind to accept potential solutions. Meditation became a gateway to receiving answers. Through a conscious connection with the whole, I learned to listen and trust in my higher self.

Meditation became my morning ritual. After a 5 a.m. doggie walk with Lucky, a twenty-minute stretch for him, fresh clean sea air for me, I settled in, tuning out the physical world, tuning into the conscious whole.

During the initial weeks of learning to calm my mind, I kept a meditation journal. I jotted notes on whatever seemed of significance as it popped into my mind, understood or not, to contemplate at a later date. I found myself rereading what I wrote every couple of weeks. What I came to recognize very quickly was a connection with my sister Jeannie.

Statements from her heart to mine guided me in times of indecision. That it was her was without question as phrases and words only she would have shared came to mind, along with answers.

Here is a classic example of how she worked with me. One morning as I meditated, I sent forth a question regarding my intimate life with Jack. It was an issue which had caused concern for quite some time. An answer came with such clarity, almost with force, it shocked me. That the words came from Jeannie, her words, her verbiage, seemed impossible.

How would she know? We never discussed my concerns. Jeannie, this answer cannot be from you...yet it feels like you...sounds like you. Jeannie, is that really you?

Suddenly the phrase 'blue moon bathrobe' popped into my head. Blue moon bathrobe.

Jeannie had made our mom a bathrobe for Christmas one year. It was a deep midnight blue; a nighttime blue. Her fleecy warm robe was adorned with yellow smiling moon faces and white stars. I found myself laughing out loud at the clarity of her message. Blue moon bathrobe. Yep, that's you Jeannie!

* * *

"Gratitude unlocks the fullness of life. It turns what we have into enough, and more. It turns denial into acceptance, chaos into order, confusion into clarity...It turns problems into gifts, failures into success, the unexpected into perfect timing, and mistakes into important events. Gratitude makes sense of our past, brings peace for today and creates a vision for tomorrow." ~ Melody Beattie

Gazing into the heavens those mornings, I came to understand that of the lessons learned since that summer of 2011, the most profound was the practice of conscious gratitude. My third step I suppose.

I find myself overjoyed at the simplicity and happiness

which has become my life. When I take the time to thank the Universe for all I know is coming my way, trust and expect that everything is happening just at it should be, life becomes elegantly simple. I feel blessed each and every day.

I suppose I have decided to share this with you now as the time on the meseta was intensely personal for me. Those early mornings staring into the vast heavens above, heavens dotted with glittering stars, brought peace and tranquility. They brought a sense of oneness with the Universal whole and a reminder that I AM connected...now and forever.

"We come spinning out of nothingness, scattering stars like dust." ~ Rumi

CHAPTER FOURTEEN

Angel in Pink

"We can all be angels to one another. We can choose to obey the still small stirring within, the little whisper that says, Go. Ask. Reach out. Be an answer to someone's plea. You have a part to play. Have faith." ~ Joan Wester Anderson

On the morning we walked into Leon, an arduous walk through an industrial area which did nothing for the soul, a walk that seems to go on for eternity, my spirits began to sink. I had been tired in the past twenty-three days, blistered toes had cried to be released from my boots at times, but this day was different. For the first time in twenty-three days, my mind and body took over... this whole trek was in question.

My decision to walk the famed Camino Frances, a centuries old pilgrimage trail leading from the village of St. Jean Pied de Port in the French Pyrenees to Santiago de Compostela, believed burial site of St. James the Apostle in the northeast of Spain, had been made two years prior. Not even a conscious decision, it had been a *soul knowing* that I was to make this remarkable journey. That my twenty-year marriage had recently ended convinced me even further that the Universe was in action and timing was exactly as it was meant. I did not believe in coincidence.

Twenty-three days of joyous camaraderie with fellow pilgrims I met along the way had been coupled at times with exhaustion and physical ache, but nothing that had dampened my exuberant spirit. I held an unfaltering belief that I was exactly where I was meant to be. Until now.

What the hell am I doing? Maybe if I hadn't embarked on this trek Jack and I would still be together. Perhaps we would have found a way to hold on to all that was good...all that was precious with our marriage...perhaps we could have let the rest go.

It is said that one's true Camino begins after the walk is finished...when *real life* kicks in again. I was aware that my *true* Camino began when I had decided to allow growth in my beliefs. My Camino began in the summer of 2011, the summer I recognized my marriage was doomed without a change. The summer in Rovinj I began reading and practicing new ways of viewing my world.

On this particular day, two years later, twenty-three

days into my trek, I found myself questioning...doubting.

Why am I walking this path...what is it I am supposed to learn? Why is my life purpose not yet clear? Damn it. Isn't that why I am here? Why do my stupid feet hurt so terribly? Where is the sense of joy and freedom I've had? Is it time to stop and recognize that perhaps my head tricked me into taking this walk and it had nothing to do with soul knowledge at all?

All morning I found myself plagued with not only the physical toll of the Camino on the body, but the soul searching that walking 800 kilometers of thought and memories will bring about.

We had only been on the road for about four hours on this twenty-third day. Not even beyond the hours of mid-day sun, when muscles and feet rebelled, yet the tears found their way from somewhere so deep inside I felt I would drown. They remained trapped, would not break free; they welled up, choked my heart, my throat...pooled...stuck.

Trudging through traffic, the stagnant air felt thick, dirty. Faces I passed were no longing smiling and wishing a cheery "Buen Camino." Empty faces devoid of emotion. I found myself so sad. Sad for my lost marriage; sad for Jack. I was sad with the knowledge that when this Camino was finished, I would return to the States, leaving behind a way of life in Spain that I had come to love. My heart ached real-izing that dear friendships would die away; that is what happens in divorce.

If I could just cry. Walk, head down, and let my tears drop to this dusty street. I know tears would help; I know they cleanse and allow life to move forward. If I could cry I could empty my heart.

Instead, my body simply ached with weight of my pack and with the weight of the tears that refused to flow.

As we neared a local cafe, I gave in and asked the others to stop for a short break.

No questions asked, backpacks and walking poles were dropped alongside a concrete bench just outside the door. *We have been together twenty-four hours a day for twenty-three days. They know me; they recognize I am in pain, physically and emotionally.*

"Cappuccino? Coke Light? What do you need, Kate? We will get it. You sit, take your boots off, we'll go in."

Crumpled on the bench, head in hands, blistered toes exposed unceremoniously to the air on the outskirts of industrial Leon, I suddenly heard a soft feminine voice greet me.

"Buenas Dias," the voice offered.

Lifting my head slightly in polite recognition of the greeting, I looked directly into the mahogany eyes of an elderly Spanish woman dressed immaculately in a light pink Sunday suit. Her dark, lustrous hair was coiffed to perfection and the pearls around her neck shone in the sun. Her smile was so intensely warm that I felt I had always known this woman.

In a voice quiet, yet projecting confident strength, she spoke in *Madriano*, high proper Spanish. I understood little in terms of the words, but I understood completely in spirit. This elegant woman asked if I was walking the Camino and from which town I had started.

"Yes, yes we are. We are walking the entire Camino Frances from St. Jean."

With this, the woman smiled and began to tell her own tale. Her Camino of many years before.

Through words, deeply held emotion and animated gestures, she explained how she had walked to Santiago de Compostela while very ill in her early twenties. Her motions led me to understand she had had a tumor somewhere in her abdomen area, but that she had walked this path in faith, believing that upon reaching the tomb of St. James in Santiago, she would be healed. Her words, warm, full of faith, unquestionable trust in why and where she had been headed, spoke directly to my heart.

And here she was, this elegant woman, on the very day of my questioning spirit. She was healthy, remarkably beautiful, and standing before me encouraging me to go on and to *trust* that I would be fine. That I was walking this Camino as I was supposed to and to not question. Before the woman turned to leave, she looked directly in my eyes, hugged me warmly, held my hands gently and said,

"Buen Camino. Buen suerte." And she was gone.

Walking partners still in the cafe, it seemed that time

had stopped. This elegant woman had somehow reached inside my being and lifted away every hurt, every sadness. I was overcome with a sense of peace and well-being. In those brief moments, my Spanish angel in a soft pink Sunday suit brought me back to my soul's knowledge that all would be well. I was *exactly* where I was supposed to be and the woman's presence at that moment, just as I needed her most, was proof...no coincidence.

Not once after that encounter did I ever question my walk. Not once after that encounter did my blistered feet feel so tender and sore, my shoulders or back ache from the weight of my pack. My Angel in Pink had touched me with energy meant to heal body and soul.

As my pilgrimage continued, I found myself deeply grateful for this remarkable gift. My belief in my soul's knowledge and learning to trust in that knowledge— believing I was exactly where I was meant to be in this life— had returned strong and intact.

I recognized that although we may not always see clearly the reasons events happen as they do, life will unfold as it is meant. Choosing to live in gratitude and expecting miracles allows the energies of the Universe to conspire on our behalf. And Angels can and will appear along the way!

CHAPTER FIFTEEN

Cruz de Ferro

*"Forgiveness is a gift to yourself. It frees you
from the past, past experiences and past relation-
ships. It allows you to live in the present time.
When you forgive yourself and forgive
others you are indeed free." ~ Louise Hay*

"Don't let it touch the floor," our therapist had in-
structed years earlier, as she dropped a crisp, white
sheet of paper.

I reached out, palm upwards, to support the drifting
sheet and was met with Jack's thumb and forefinger taking
hold of only the smallest bit of the closest corner as it floated past.

"This paper is your marriage," she cautioned us.

The evening before the climb to Cruz de Ferro, I sat

95

contemplating the enormous weight of the day ahead. Cruz de Ferro has been a sacred site on the Camino Frances for over one thousand years. This highest of elevations on the pilgrimage path is the site of the famed Iron Cross.

Standing atop a mound of rocks, rocks placed by thousands of pilgrims before me, the Cruz de Ferro reaches to the heavens above. This is the site at which I had known for months I would leave my gratitude rock. My rock, a symbol of gratitude and grace for the abundance in my life, would be left as a thank you for my many blessings. And it would be left as a symbol of letting go of a troubled marriage while simultaneously being thankful for every good thing this union brought to my world.

Yet, the evening before this ascent, I found myself compelled to write. Once, the leaving of my rock felt perfect...like 'enough.' Now I was pulled to write a note releasing blame, a note of forgiveness to Jack. Our years together, glorious in so many aspects, also brought heartache and emptiness to us both. Sitting quietly, away from the camaraderie of the others, I found a few moments of solitude. This writing was important. The words I would leave behind must portray exactly the emotions swirling through me. *Would it be so simple? Is that all truly it takes...just let go...release the hurt and choose to move forward?*

The next day's climb was long and arduous. With heads bent against a constant wall of wind and drizzle, I questioned whether we would make it through. Perhaps ending our day early at the local *albergue* we visited for a quick sandwich stop would be wiser. Start again in early morning light.

Checking route maps once more, we opted to push ahead knowing we could reach overnight accommodations before dark if we moved as quickly as possible to our main destination. Cruz de Ferro. The anticipation of reaching the summit was palpable.

This place, a hallowed ground of troubles and strife left behind, was calling to us. Wet weather gear flapping in the wind we continued up the long winding road. Reaching the top we would stand at 4,750 feet in altitude. The highest point on our journey, we would be at the crest of the Rabanal Pass through the Montes de Leon.

Rounding a final bend in the road, a tour bus sat rumbling, exhaust polluting the crisp mountain air. *Please...please don't let this site have become a tourist trap.*

Disappointment and despair. These are the only words to describe the sudden sadness I felt. A moment I had anticipated for months vanished in a fog of diesel fumes.

Whatever my expectations, I knew I must allow and accept the sight before me—it was not going to change. Cruz de Ferro belonged to everyone, pilgrims trudging for miles on foot and those who arrived by the ease of bus and car. I could choose disappointment or I could choose gratitude for the very ability I had allowing me to trudge for miles. Choose Grace; choose Gratitude. Cruz de Ferro, at that unexpected moment, began teaching. A lesson in the release of expectations was there for me to claim or reject.

As I climbed the four plus meters high mound of rocks, wandering the circumference to find the perfect location to leave my gratitude rock, a sense of calm embraced me. Glancing up to survey the area, I realized everyone other than our small group had left. Cruz de Ferro was ours. The sun, hidden in rain clouds for most of the day, was shining warmth over the surrounding grounds.

With a prayer of thanks for the joy of this Camino and the blessings bestowed on me these last years, I lovingly placed my gratitude rock on the pile. Tears flowed as a sense of release came over me. The lightness of spirit I had anticipated soaked every cell of my being as I stood breathing in a loving energy.

And now to lay down my note of forgiveness, tucked away deep in a jacket pocket, waiting for perfect placement. Across the grassy walkway a tiny grey stone chapel caught my eye. Without question I knew this was where I would leave my note.

Standing outside the wrought iron window bars, paint cracked and peeling, I peered into the darkened space. Simple unlit candles adorned the altar; no gilded statues, no arches reaching to heaven. With a prayer of love, I wiggled my hand through the narrow bars gently releasing written words, watching them float to the stone floor below. Sorrow. Tears of love, anger, blame and pain finally loose and flooding my cheeks. Words so carefully crafted the evening before floated away. A simple statement:

Jack, I release all blame. I release blaming you. You are forgiven. I am letting go now.

Outside the wrought iron window bars of the chapel at Cruz de Ferro, sacred site of leaving worries and troubles behind, I once again watched as a crisp white piece of paper drifted. This time it touches the ground. This time I knew I was not meant to save it. I am meant to let it fall away. There is something more waiting...calling for me.

The air was eerily quiet as my group and I took time to contemplate the experience before moving on. Each in our own worlds, we sat distanced, spread out across the grassy lawn. Sacred ground saturated with centuries of pilgrim tears welcomed us home.

With a knowing welling from deep within, that *soul knowledge* I have come to trust, I stared up at the bare iron cross high above me. A whisper of love so gentle cradled my heart. In that wondrous moment a final absolution to myself

Kate, I release you of blame. You are forgiven.

From this moment on, I will remember him only in love. Healing begins.

CHAPTER SIXTEEN

Sarria

"The reason it hurts so much to separate is because our souls are connected." ~ Nicholas Sparks

Waving goodbye as they continued on to Portomarin, I stood on the corner wondering which way to turn. My Camino family of thirty-two days moved on, waving walking sticks high in the air.

"Buen Camino, Kate! See you in Santiago."

In Sarria, I spent a night alone; the first night alone in six months. The prospect of precious hours of privacy, hours so longed for these past weeks, was now met with trepidation. Alone.

Do I even remember how to do alone?

My compatriots had been with me for the last four and a half weeks. Day after day, night after night, we shared stories, fears, marriages and children. We lived together twenty-four hours a day sharing meals, bunk rooms, clothes washing duties and shower facilities. Teeth were brushed side by side in communal dormitory bathrooms. Trees protecting the view from the road had been guarded as Mother Nature called when no bathrooms were available. Other pilgrims came and went in our group, but the core remained. In many ways, I knew Paul and Guy, my smoked salmon Camino brothers, better than I knew many life-long friends. Thirty-two days.

They knew me. They had watched as tears rolled down my cheeks, my side aching from the joy of laughter. Mornings of private contemplation had been honored as I walked ahead, lost in thoughts...memories. Sunrise hours; dedicated to listening to all the Universe was trying to teach me.

These men watched my heart hurt when I finally shared the tale of my broken marriage...the marriage I refused to let go for so very long. A marriage I intuitively knew had become no more than a loving friendship years before. Thirty-two days and my soul had been bared to strangers who became my support network...my Camino family. In Sarria we parted, if only for a few days, yet my soul knew this sacred time together had come to an end.

Liz was due to return the next morning. She would walk the final 120 kilometers of this Camino with me. Together we would triumphantly march into Santiago. Her first ten days coupled with the next five earned her the coveted *compostele,* the certificate recognizing completion of the

120 required kilometers. Obligations at home had pulled her away after the first ten days on the trail. The next day she would return. For that one night I was alone.

A glass of local Albariño wine and a cozy bed in a simple well-kept hotel—bliss! I chose to stay in. I opened my notebook. A page of notes written six months earlier slipped out. Barely legible words, handwritten emotions, spilled across the page.

It had been April, some five and a half months earlier, when the suggestion "counseling and self-help books" had instead led to divorce. I read my words, trying to remember the feelings of those days. Words of fear, anger...feelings of guilt and sorrow stared at me.

Reading what my heart knew then, I found myself quietly smiling. Only a few months later and those words no longer broke my spirit. Those words told of hidden truths in our marriage; truths having hinted at the troubles to come for many years. But they were simply that...words of fact.

As I read them that evening, I felt such a deep compassion for Jack, for us. Anger, fear...all emotions of the past. This Camino, one I knew I must take even though not understanding why, had allowed me to walk away. Truly lay down blame and guilt. A night alone for the first time in months, with no distractions in which to hide, was my proof. That I felt at peace, warmed in a deep sense of gratitude and love, was my proof. I drifted off. Happy.

Liz took the train into Sarria. Waiting outside the hotel the next morning I anxiously watched taxi cabs round the corner, excited to see her face and continue on together with stories to tell. It was only mid-morning so we started our walk within an hour. A quick cleanup in the hotel for her, I checked out, and we were on our way. Five and a half days until Santiago.

As always when friends reunite, the conversation turns to home, family and local gossip.

As we walked the next few days, sharing my adventures of the past few weeks along with her tales of the local home life, I found my sleep beginning to fade away at night. Memories battled for position. In the chit chat of family and friends, there was, of course, talk of him.

Jack is a part of Moraira's daily life. We have been a group of eight for over two years. Four couples in Moraira, fast friends. Liz and her husband along with Jack and I were part of an expat family of eight. His name was, naturally, as much a part of conversation as any other.

I had left him, us, behind. My days had been calm. Serene. The journey had been filled with nothing other than hours joy since releasing my note of forgiveness at Cruz de Ferro. *Why does a simple mention of his name bring such sadness especially when the sun goes down?*

Three days later we sat a local cafe having late night cocktails. Two more days and we would reach Santiago. Thirty-five days on the Camino was coming to an end...*then what?* For that evening, I forgot the questions swirling in my brain and enjoyed the village life.

We watched children dance and play beneath broadleaf shade trees in the plaza. Cool evening air brought locals out for ice cream and a stroll. Strings of multi-colored lights adorned plaza cafes. Menu boards propped against a nearby tree beckoned diners. Tranquility.

Sipping a second brandy, a heartache I had not felt since Cruz de Ferro was now back and finding its way to my cheeks. In the midst of a cooled Spanish evening in a tiny town somewhere on the ancient pilgrimage trail that is the Camino, Liz held onto my hands tightly as she watched my shoulders tremble.

That dull gripping ache which wrenches at a broken heart when memories flood the spirit had returned. The yearning for what once was held me captive as tears slipped onto the crumpled worn tablecloth.

It wasn't over.

CHAPTER SEVENTEEN

Santiago de Compostela

*"When I let go of what I am,
I become what I might be." ~ Lao Tzu*

The mood on the final morning was electric! Pilgrims at our *albergue* ate a hurried breakfast and headed out into the predawn dark. Headlamps lit the way as the day started on this final push. By noon most of us would be in Santiago de Compostela. Shouts of "Buen Camino" echoed along the path as walkers passed by, strides longer, gaits faster than in the previous weeks. The energy was palpable, invigorating. Leaving the final kilometers behind, we raced to make the traditional pilgrim's Mass at the famed Cathedral de Santiago. Joy at the completion of the task mixed with sorrow at knowing this simple life would soon end.

These last weeks had been days of serene simplicity. Walk, rest, eat, sleep, walk, rest. I was a pilgrim with a pack and nothing more. Meals had been hearty, filled with the starches needed to keep energy strong. Plates of seasoned rice or warm buttered pasta, rich bean and lentil soups, lean pork or roasted chicken and *pan*, bread, always baskets of heavy homemade bread. Beds had been simple, a place to lay your weary head, relax your tired shoulders.

On that final day, we all realized our journey would soon come to an end. I felt a quiet sense of mourning the loss of these remarkable days conflicting with a joyous anticipation. Knowing that Mass would wait until the next day for me, I relaxed into the final stretch. Our greeting committee, friends from Moraira, would be waiting somewhere inside the main gates as we arrived.

After a few hours, we made it to the top of Mount Gozo, which was the last climb before Santiago de Compostela. Standing atop the mountain, we took a well-earned break, leaning on walking sticks as we stared over the sprawling, modern urban city below. It occurred to me that in a short while I would have walked just under 500 miles. The words to a Peter, Paul and Mary 60s folk song played through my head until I just had to sing out loud.

"Lord I'm one, Lord I'm two, Lord I'm three, Lord I'm four. Lord I'm 500 miles away from home."

Staring down upon the famous city, we saw the Cathedral spires marking its epicenter. When we reach the center, the cathedral will mark the moment of completion of our pilgrimage to Santiago de Compostela, the third most famous pilgrimage in Christianity. Two hours at best and this journey of a lifetime would come to its close.

We began the trek down Mount Gozo and into town. It was laboriously slow. Anticipation, which has been simmering for weeks, was now at full boil; excitement overflowed. Pilgrims laughed and called out to each other when we finally entered the newer urban city boundaries, passing by the enormous steel structured sign that marked the entrance of the Santiago de Compostela city limits. Modern, somewhat garish in its metal construction, it was still a magnificent prize—the trophy of victory. We had arrived.

Photographs marked the achievement as pilgrims, familiar faces and strangers alike, took turns memorializing this occasion for each other. Cameras, iPhones, iPads—all at the ready. All testifying that we were here. We made this trek, we lived this life, and none of us will ever be the same.

Walking into town, a young woman with matted dreadlocks piled high on her head, wearing once brilliantly colored attire now faded in sun and dust, asked if she could walk with me. She had come from Barcelona, she said. She camped all the way, traveling on little financial resources. Her parents were so deeply disappointed in her choice to leave college. Unsure of which way life would take her, she opted for a pilgrimage to try to settle her mind, to find herself. Although she made fellow pilgrim friendships along the way, on this day—the one most important—she found herself alone. Her experience, one she had attempted to make as authentic as possible, was now reaching its end.

As we headed toward the center of the city, the old town of Santiago, she hoped to walk through the gates and celebrate with fellow pilgrims. At twenty-three, she was younger than my son. Feeling her energy, her exuberance, the mother in me told her how proud I would be of her decision to follow her heart song...make her pilgrimage...try to find her way in this world in a manner that speaks solely to her. She reached over and squeezed my hand with her toughened skin. It was a hand that knew a challenged pilgrimage. I was her new Camino family for the next few blocks...a Mom giving approval of her right to choose her own destiny.

We chatted away, comparing Camino notes, laughing at silly occurrences along the way. And then with a brief kiss on the cheek she was gone, lost in the throng of pilgrims jostling to cross the busy roundabouts, rushing to the finish.

It is said that to each person we meet on our journey through this life, we hold one of three positions: we are Teacher, we are Student, and sometimes, we are both. It occurs to me that when the energies of the Universe bring two people together for the briefest of times and one, if not both, leave the encounter far richer in spirit, perhaps then we, in our earthly bodies, act as Angels...givers of guidance...channelers of love. Much as my Angel in Pink in Leon blessed me with a deep soul knowing that I could and would make it through this trek, I am deeply moved by the few moments shared with a young pilgrim from Barcelona and trust that perhaps, in those moments I was able to pay forward the gift of love...that she felt blessed by me.

Arriving

Down crowded alleyways, following the final yellow arrow markers of the Camino trek, we rounded corners straining to see the plaza which marks the point where five separate pilgrimage routes through Spain and Portugal join. Routes that have brought pilgrims to this sacred place for centuries merge just inside crumbled city walls.

There was the fountain! I had seen it in photographs. This fountain marks the merge of all five routes, the entrance to the most ancient and sacred road in all of Santiago. Odd, it looked and felt so simple, unceremonious. My expectations had been of medieval grandeur, a celebrated entry through rounded arched gateways of old. Five hundred miles later and we entered what could have been any other Spanish city. I felt a momentary disillusionment, and then the excitement of having reached this point bubbled.

Somewhere close, friends from Moraira were waiting to welcome us. This joyous reunion had been planned for months. They are family here to greet us, celebrate our achievement.

As we crossed the plaza, my friends positioned me slightly ahead.

"YOU lead us in. You have walked the entire Camino from St Jean. We will follow you! You have earned this—

go!"

My entire body shook. Overjoyed at reaching Santiago after nearly 800 kilometers, exhausted from battling the mixed emotions of the last several days, excited tears flowed freely through my laughter. I looked across the plaza and caught the faces of our loved ones. There they were! Jumping and waving wildly, they hollered our names at full volume.

Suddenly my knees grew weak, buckling. Through the masses of arriving pilgrims and onlookers, Jack stood to greet us.

In a single moment, memories of joyful times flashed through my mind playing like scenes of life flashing before death. Laughing, crying, I walked straight to him. He was here. He came. In disbelief, I readied myself to be wrapped in his arms, welcomed with the love of twenty years. *Why else would he be here but to tell me he has changed his mind, he wants a life together?*

A hug, arms stiff...cold and impersonal...welcomed me to Santiago.

Why is he here?

Rounding corners as we all marched toward the Cathedral, the moment I could truly claim to have completed this journey, familiar faces were everywhere. Calls of greeting rang out...pilgrims ran swooping each other into jubilant hugs.

Exuberance at completing this sacred trek carried me

through the afternoon into an evening of revelry. Throughout the remainder of the afternoon and evening, wine flowed. We relaxed with each other, Jack and I, laughing with the others, trying. Our shoulders touched as the evening drew late; a familiar comfort wrapped me. He held my hand. The young girl in me was thrilled at his touch. Inhibitions weakened with wine, I invited him back to my room. His nearness captivated me; he has always been the only man I wanted.

"I have my own room," he stated, pecking me on the cheek. He said his goodnights to the others and walked away.

CHAPTER EIGHTEEN

Finisterre

"Surrender to what is, let go of what was and have faith in what will be." ~ *Sonia Ricotti*

Santiago de Compostela - compostela, field of stars. Lying awake most of the night, I found myself staring out the small monastery window allowing fresh night air into my hotel room. Gazing at stars above on this clear lovely night, I relived the last months of our life together.

That Jack would join the others on this three-day sojourn to Santiago for the welcoming of Liz and I was not a surprise. It was a party after all and he was not one to miss a celebration! Perhaps the others felt his being there would rekindle our marriage.

"See? He came; he cares. You two need to get back together!"

With a bit of coaxing by the gals and some ribbing by

the guys, they would have convinced him to join. That I, on the emotional high of a thirty-seven-day walk completed, with a heart no longer feeling resentment and blame, would see his presence as a possible signal of something more was understandable. That the two of us, wine infused, would let down our guards and actually enjoy each other's company for the evening could be seen as expected. And, that we slept in separate rooms in separate hotels, well, even though I felt such humiliation at his rejection, we both understood.

Strange how the scenes of our lives replay. Different stages, yet the content repeats itself.

A field of stars through the wrought iron bars of a tiny monastery room. Cold stone walls. Once again, a call to release. Just as the tiny stone chapel at Cruz de Ferro had accepted my note of forgiveness weeks before, these monastery walls would accept my tears. I felt a call for forgiveness. I drifted to sleep, mascara smeared cotton pillowcases absorbing my sorrow.

The morning sun streaked through gauze curtains awakening me to a new day, a fresh beginning. On this pivotal day, in the Holy city of Santiago de Compostela, I would say goodbye. Heartache was replaced with a quiet peace; a feeling of compassion for this man I called my husband. I took out a photo of his face, the face I fell in love with all those year ago. Strong, confident then, now I see a vulnerable man; a little boy lost in a world he cannot face, will not allow himself to face, at all costs.

Walking Jack and our friends to the taxi stand two hours later, I turned to kiss his cheek goodbye, smiling. Only love...all that was left. Where this blessed peace came from I do not know, but I am grateful as I waved them off. They are gone.

The End of the Earth

My walking sticks tapped the sidewalk confidently as I found my way forward to Finisterre, the ancient *end of the earth*. Four days later, I stood on rugged cliffs high above the Atlantic Ocean, waves crashing on the rocks below. Staring into a vast expanse of sea and air, secluded from other pilgrims and visitors, I once again had found my way to the sea...to reflect.

One summer day over a year earlier, I had gone to the sea. I had gone there in anguish, gone to meditate. I had walked away having surrendered. That morning's events: my sister Jeannie coming to me once again, my grandparents cradling me in the spirit of their loving energy, a multitude of clouds—clouds of all dimensions and forecasts—simultaneously floating in view had shook my senses...shook me to remember what my soul knew. There is no here or there, then or now. Everything is *NOW*—and the Universe will operate on my behalf if I *allow*.

I surrender to the consciousness that I am a part of. Surrender to love. Accept what is, forget what was, and trust in what will be.

On the rocky cliffs of Finisterre, my soul spoke a truth I

had known all along, a truth the Universe had been whispering: I had to walk to this place, this ancient end of the earth, to walk away from him...to be able to start anew.

Air, fresh and clean, caressed my face. The sun shone warm on my skin. On the horizon, sky the colors of cyan blended in an azure blue sea.

Saying goodbye to Jack in Santiago...a final goodbye to a life chapter I knew I must close... opened my heart. Whispers. My soul, free from the past, was listening.

As I propped on my bed that evening against a wall of fluffed pillows, staring at swaying boats bobbing in the tiny fishing harbor, I began rereading my journaling. Words which flowed from pen to paper since that glorious morning outside Pamplona, when my sister Jeannie spoke to me, were now a message, guiding me to the next chapter of my life. As if a wall had been knocked away, a bright new world lay before me. I saw it clearly.

*"I detach myself from all preconceived outcomes
and trust that all is well."* ~ Anita Moorjani

My own words jotted over the past six weeks, reminded me that the most wondrous moments I had known on the Camino had been while actually walking. Staring at galaxies stretched out across the meseta skies. Marveling at early morning dew, shining bright on spider webs, binding grass blades. Cow bells clanging in the distance calling me to come peek over the fence, or flocks of sheep hunkered down against a brutal wind. Hot muggy days forcing the sweat to stream down my back under the bulk of a fully-laden backpack and the fresh crisp air biting at fingers and ears on those pre-dawn mountain terrain mornings. The familiar weight of my pack and tap of walking sticks...somewhere in all this is my purpose...my call. I am to walk and write. Simple. Where it will take me I am unsure, but my soul knows...just as it knew I would walk this Camino.

The Universe had been whispering and little by little over the last years I had learned to listen. Nothing in my life is out of order.

Clearly I look back several years to those summer afternoons in Rovinj immersed in the words of Dyer and Coelho and I know they were the beginning of a pilgrimage which would bring me to understand that I AM a part of a whole.

And, that when I listen carefully...when I listen with my soul...I can hear the whispers calling.

> *"Let yourself be silently drawn by the strange pull*
> *of what you really love. It will not lead you astray."*
> *~ Rumi*

EPILOGUE

*"One's destination is never a place, but a new way
of seeing things."* ~ *Henry Miller*

Eighteen months ago, I left the cliffs of Finisterre. Listening to that call in my soul, knowing I am to walk and write, I journeyed to Patagonia in February of 2015. A land that has intrigued me since childhood, in the isolated remote wilderness of windswept granite, I took the final steps to reach a state of gratitude and closure with Jack.

My beliefs allow for no coincidences. On this trek to the end of the southern world, I found myself able to accept all that has been and release the past.

Our final good-bye when I left Spain several weeks after my Camino was loving and warm. His embrace then was the embrace I had longed for when he stood to greet us as we entered the plaza that day in Santiago.

Since the end days of the Camino, I had felt a need to thank him for the gifts of our life together. Somehow following my heart and *thanking him* for that life seemed important.

Months prior, at Cruz de Ferro, I wrote words releasing blame, letting them slip to the floor of the tiny chapel on the mountain. Now I wrote a letter thanking him for the joyous moments, the love and lessons our years together brought.

The words flowed as if written by Spirit. Bliss enveloped me as I embraced genuine feelings of love and gratitude.

Now I knew I was healed.

Once again, a simple piece of crisp white paper told our story. I held it gently, tenderly, protecting a memory of love. Ready to move on.

Author Bio

Katharine Elliott left a successful thirty-year career in the hospitality industry to care for her mother-in-law as she fought her last months of a fifteen-year battle with cancer. Within two weeks of her death, Kate's middle sister was diagnosed with pancreatic cancer. Four and a half months later she took her last breath.

After the deaths, she and her husband made a bold move, followed their hearts and settled overseas to live a dream in Europe. They spent four years in a medieval Croatian village on the Adriatic, followed by a move to the Costa Blanca in Spain. In the summer of 2011, Katharine read and reread authors Wayne Dyer, Anita Moorjani, and Paulo Coelho. Focused on a new way of thinking, she embarked on a path of spiritual growth.

Following her soul's calling, Katharine walked the 800-kilometer Camino Santiago de Compostela in the fall of 2014. That journey sparked a passion for long-distance walking and a call to write. In February 2015, Katharine hiked the famed W Trek of Patagonian Chile and the renowned trails of Argentina's El Chaltan. Her next walk took her to Italy in September 2015, to trek a portion of the Via Francigena, a pilgrimage of approximately 2,000 kilometers stretching from Canterbury to Rome.

A native of the Pacific Northwest, Katharine attended Portland Community College and Portland State, studying Speech Communication and Public speaking. Katharine has one son, Gregory, a daughter-in-law, Allison, and granddaughter, Gwen Dylan Rose. Katharine's large extended family lives in the Pacific Northwest.